STAR WARS®

CLONE WARS
ADVENTURES
VOLUME 3

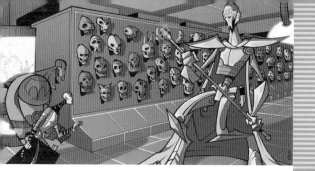

designers
Lani Schreibstein & Josh Elliott

assistant editor
Dave Marshall

editor
Jeremy Barlow

publisher
Mike Richardson

special thanks to Sue Rostoni and Amy Gary
at Lucas Licensing

talk about this book online at: *www.darkhorse.com/help/boards*

✦ The events in these stories take place approximately
six months after the Battle of Geonosis.

Advertising Sales: (503) 652-8815 x370
Comic Shop Locator Service: (888) 266-4226
DarkHorse.com
StarWars.com

ISBN 978-1-59307-307-7

9 10 8

STAR WARS: CLONE WARS ADVENTURES Volume 3, February 2005. Published by Dark Horse Comics, Inc., 10956 SE Main Street, Milwaukie, OR 97222. Star Wars © 2005 Lucasfilm Ltd. & ™. All rights reserved. Used under authorization. Text and illustrations for Star Wars are © 2005 Lucasfilm Ltd. Dark Horse Books® and the Dark Horse logo are registered trademarks of Dark Horse Comics, Inc. All rights reserved. No portion of this publication may be reproduced or transmitted, in any form or by any means, without the express written permission of Dark Horse Comics, Inc. Names, characters, places, and incidents featured in this publication either are the product of the author's imagination or are used fictitiously. Any resemblance to actual persons (living or dead), events, institutions, or locales, without satiric intent, is coincidental. Printed at 1010 Printing International, Ltd., Guangdong Province, China

STAR WARS

CLONE WARS
ADVENTURES
VOLUME 3

"ROGUE'S GALLERY"
script Haden Blackman
art The Fillbach Brothers
colors Sigmund Torre

"THE PACKAGE"
script Ryan Kaufman
art The Fillbach Brothers
colors Pamela Rambo

"A STRANGER IN TOWN"
script and art The Fillbach Brothers
colors Sno Cone Studios

"ONE BATTLE"
script Tim Mucci
art The Fillbach Brothers
colors Sigmund Torre

lettering
Michael David Thomas

cover
The Fillbach Brothers and Dan Jackson

Dark Horse Books®

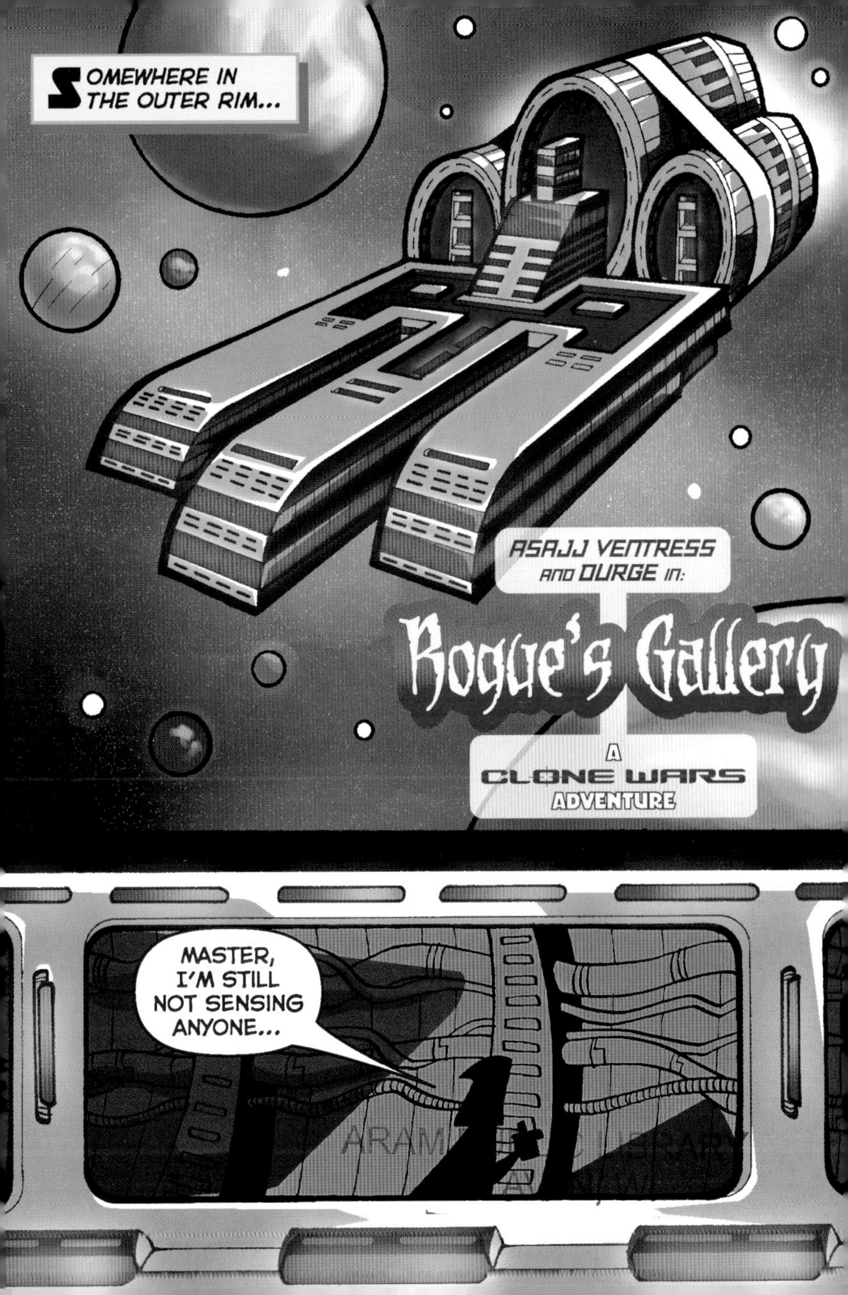
SOMEWHERE IN THE OUTER RIM...
ASAJJ VENTRESS AND DURGE IN:
Rogue's Gallery
A CLONE WARS ADVENTURE
MASTER, I'M STILL NOT SENSING ANYONE...

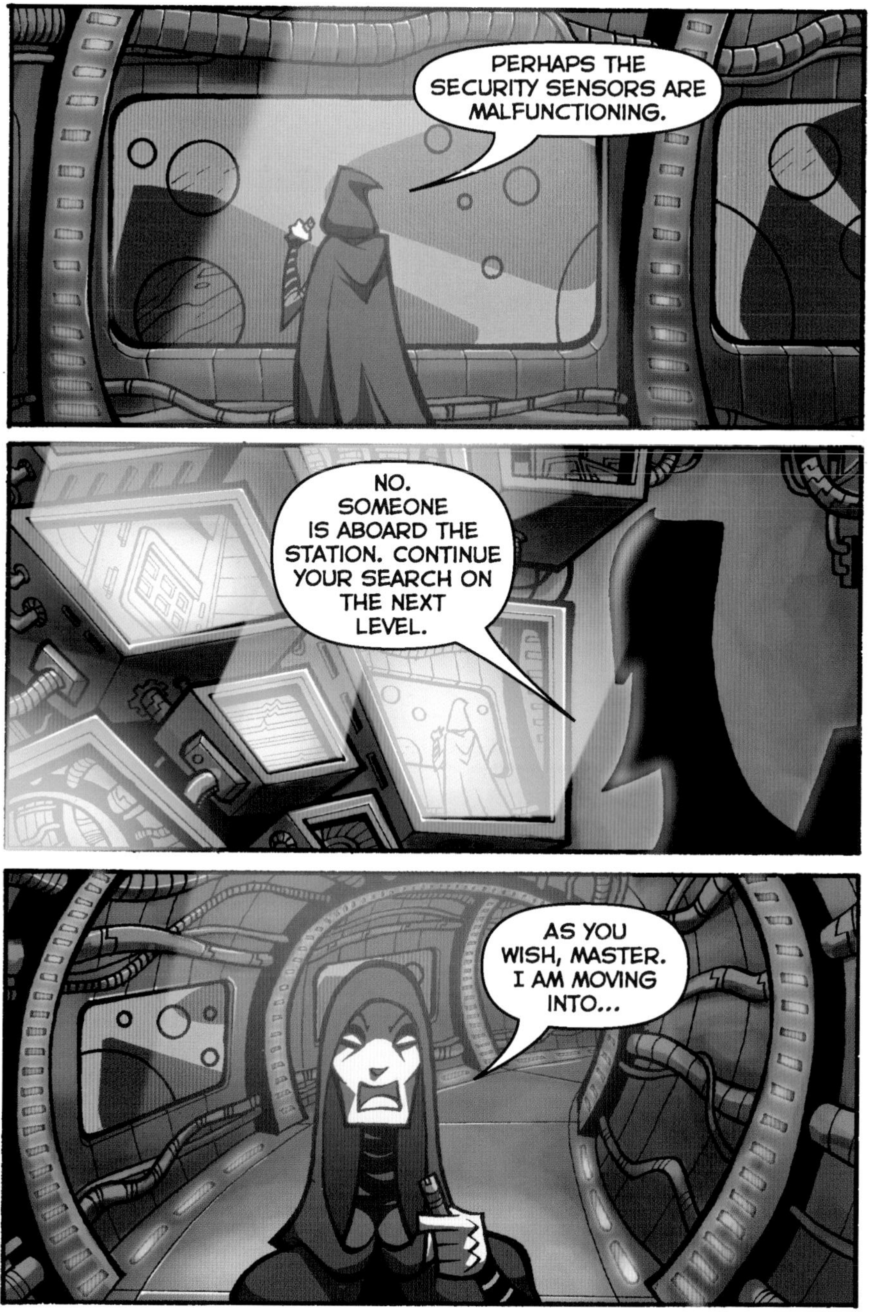
PERHAPS THE SECURITY SENSORS ARE MALFUNCTIONING.
NO. SOMEONE IS ABOARD THE STATION. CONTINUE YOUR SEARCH ON THE NEXT LEVEL.
AS YOU WISH, MASTER. I AM MOVING INTO...

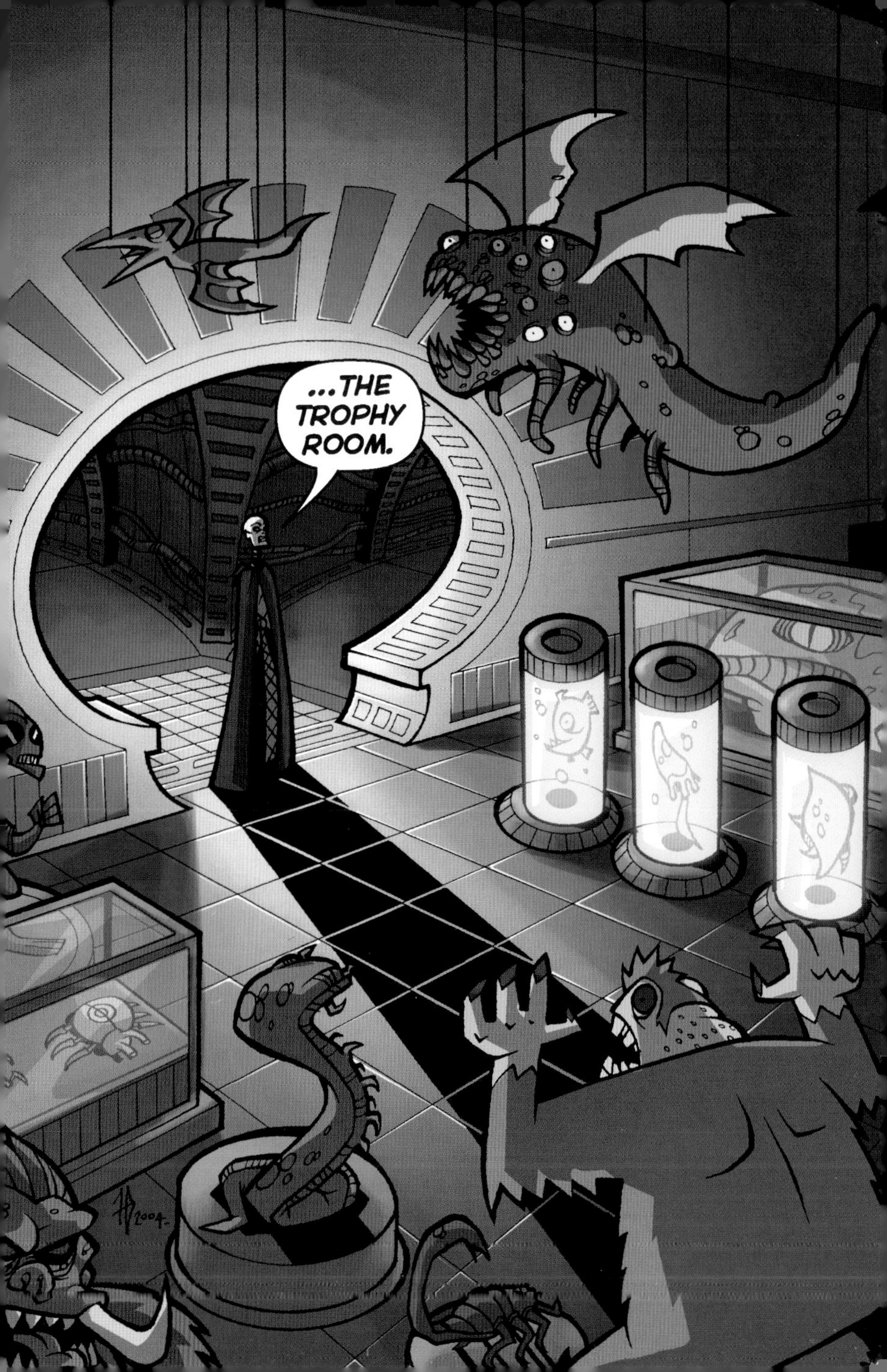
...THE TROPHY ROOM.

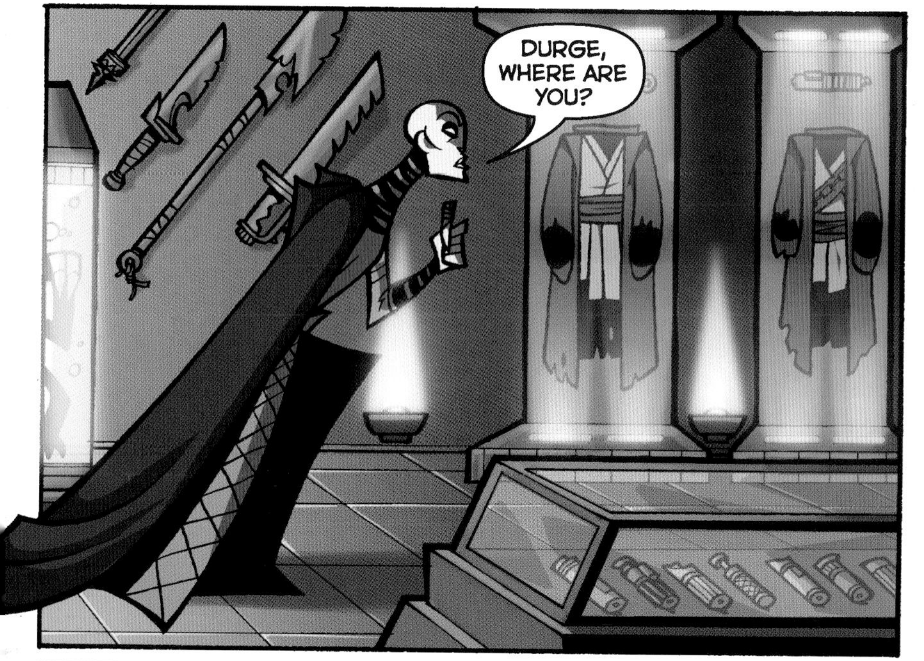
DURGE, WHERE ARE YOU?

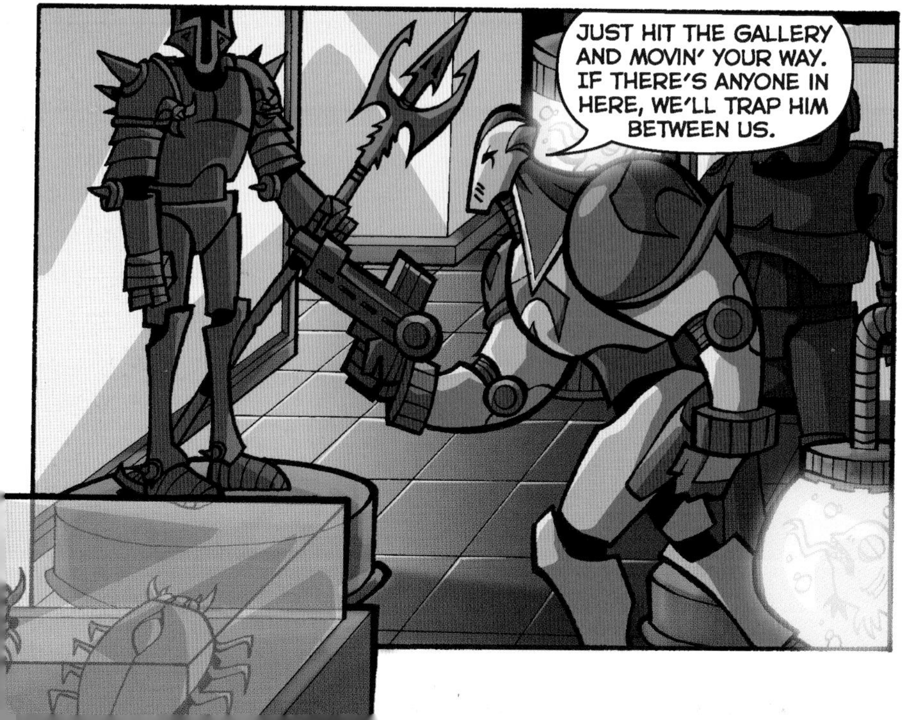
JUST HIT THE GALLERY AND MOVIN' YOUR WAY. IF THERE'S ANYONE IN HERE, WE'LL TRAP HIM BETWEEN US.

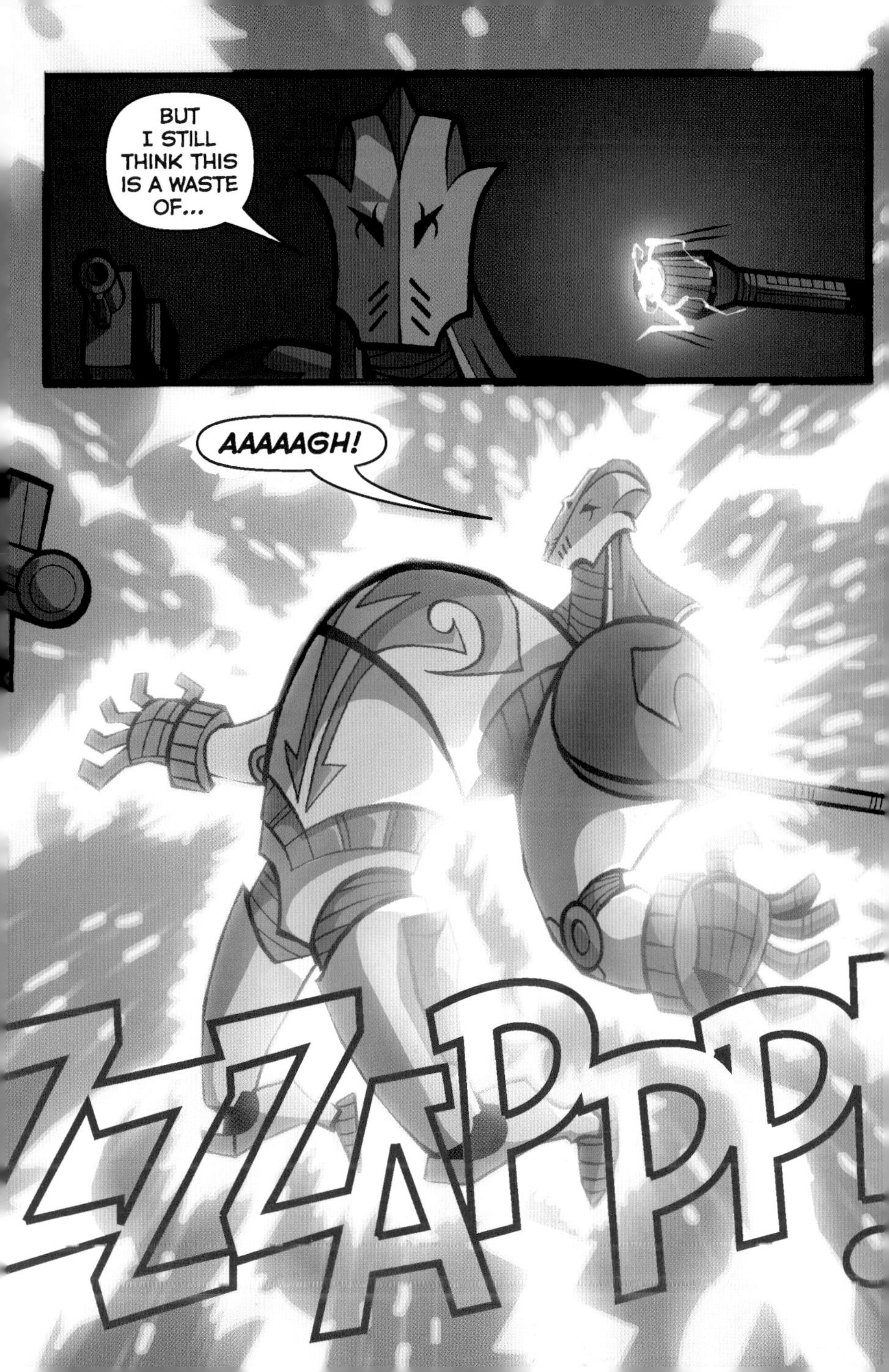
BUT I STILL THINK THIS IS A WASTE OF...
AAAAAGH!
ZZZAPPP!

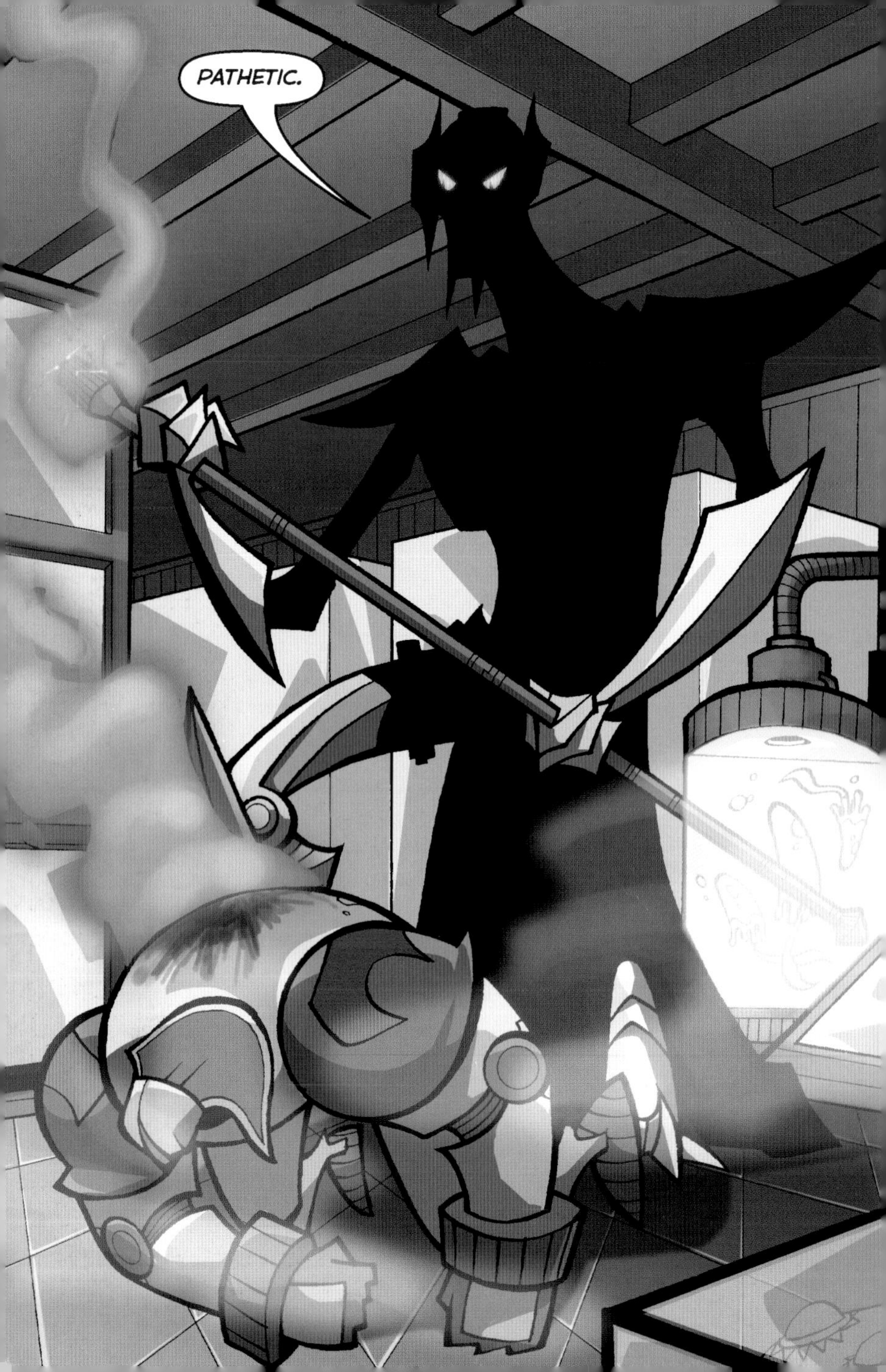
PATHETIC.

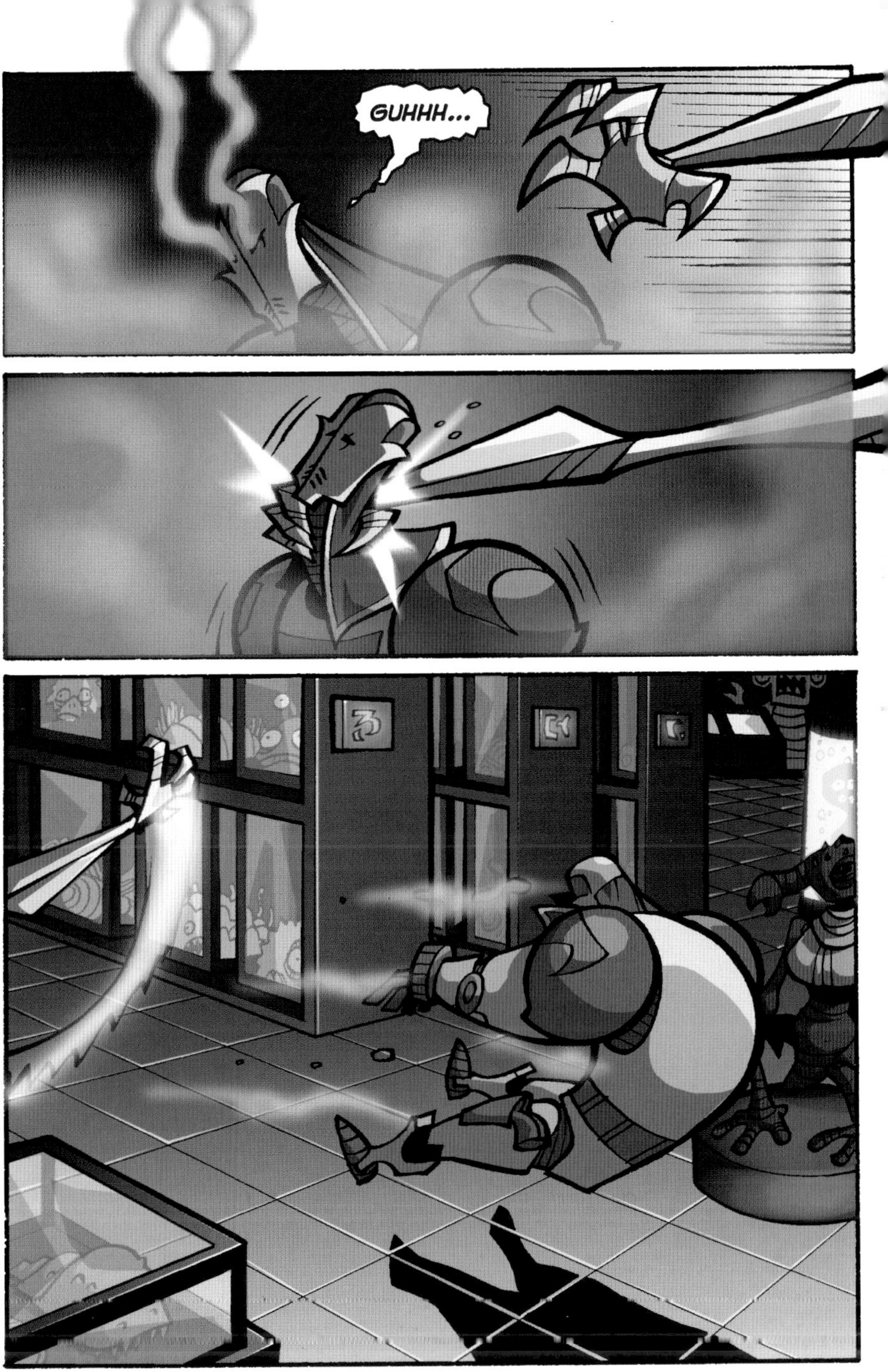
GUHHH...

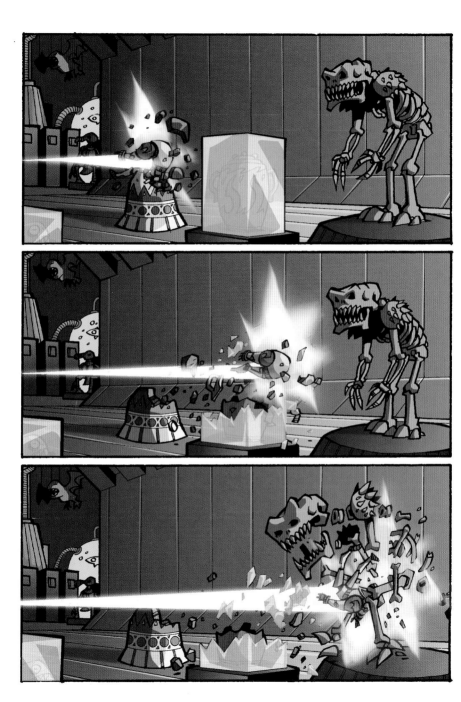

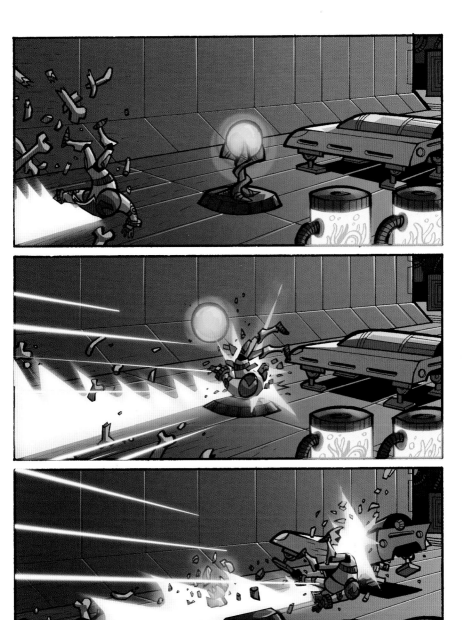

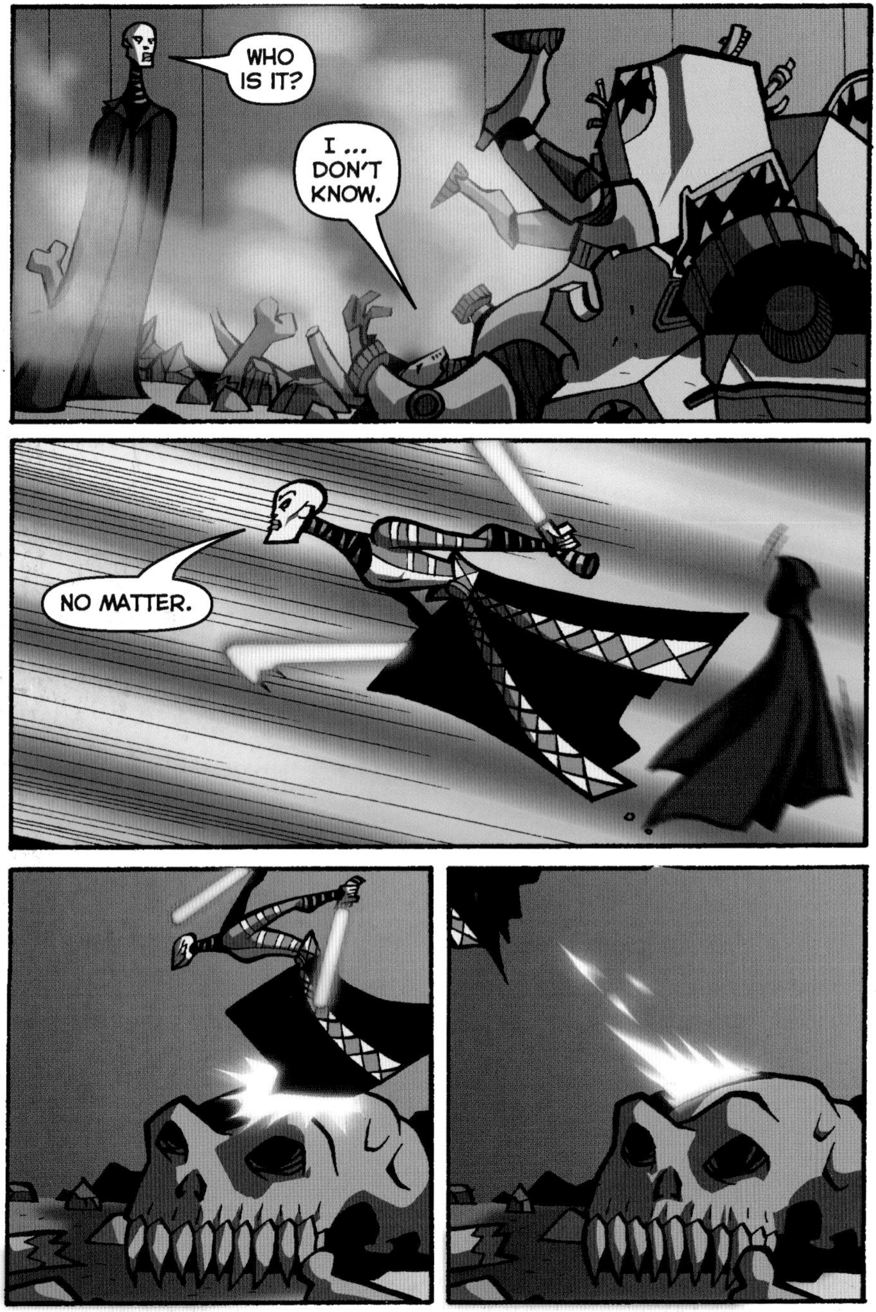
WHO IS IT?
I ... DON'T KNOW.
NO MATTER.

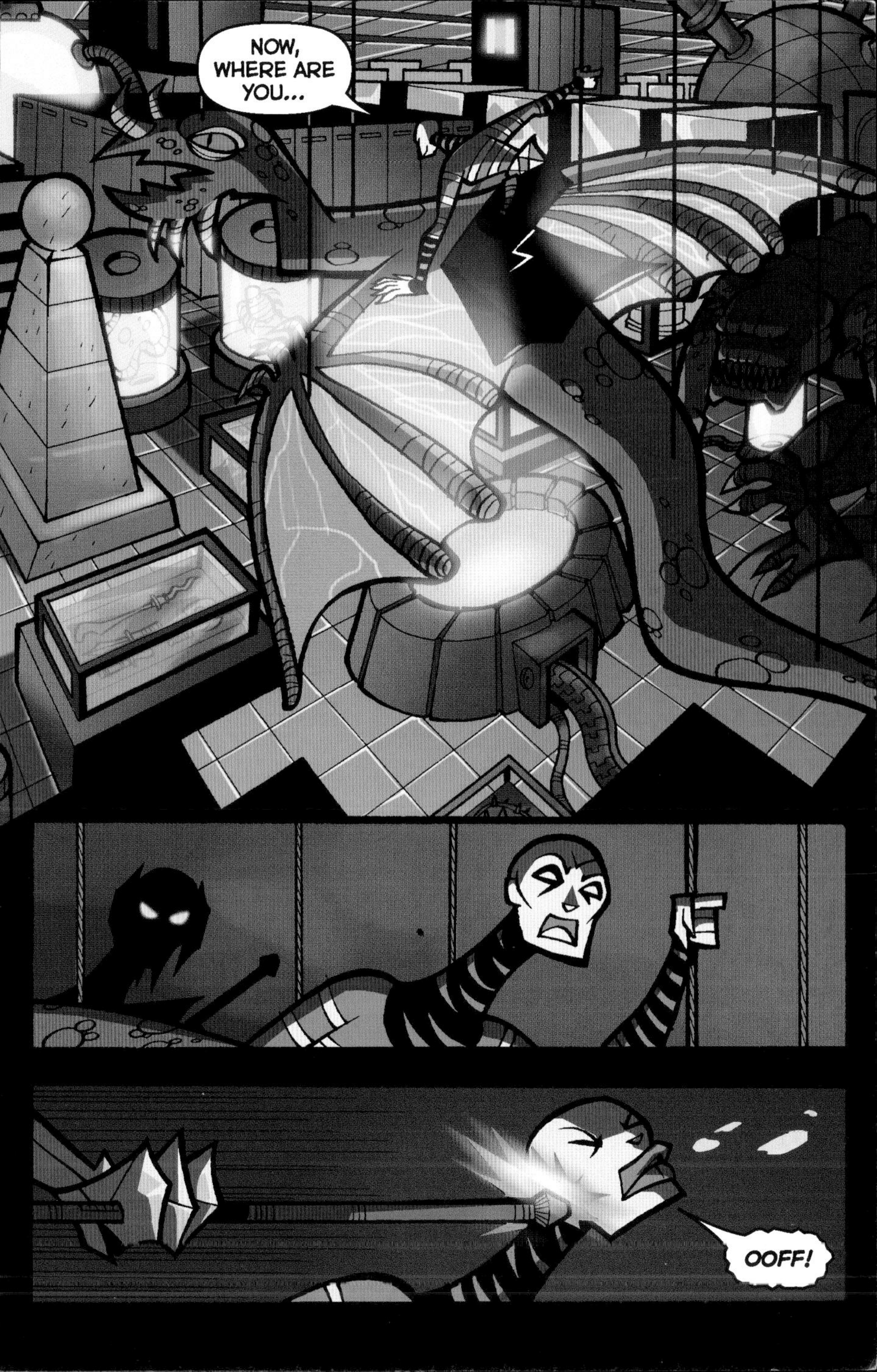
NOW, WHERE ARE YOU...
OOFF!

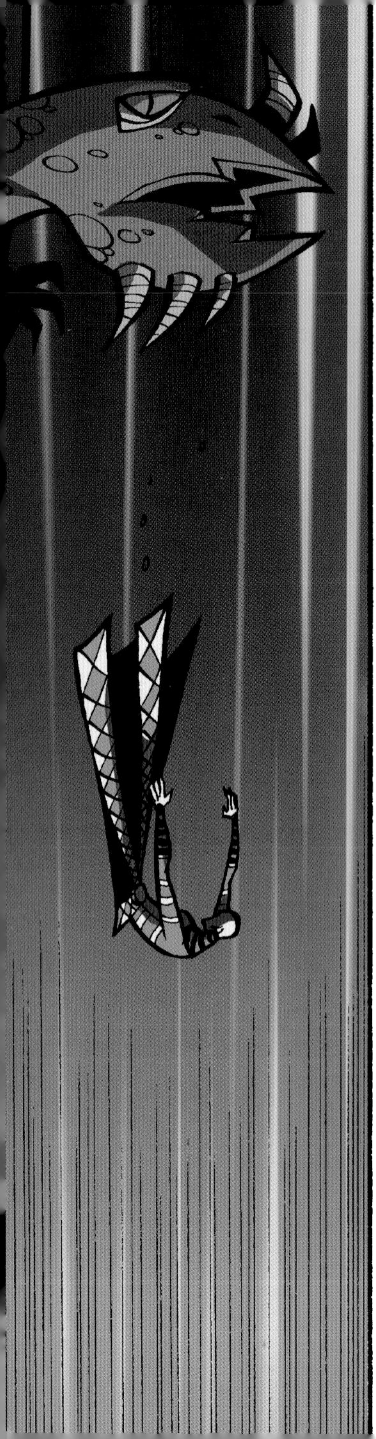
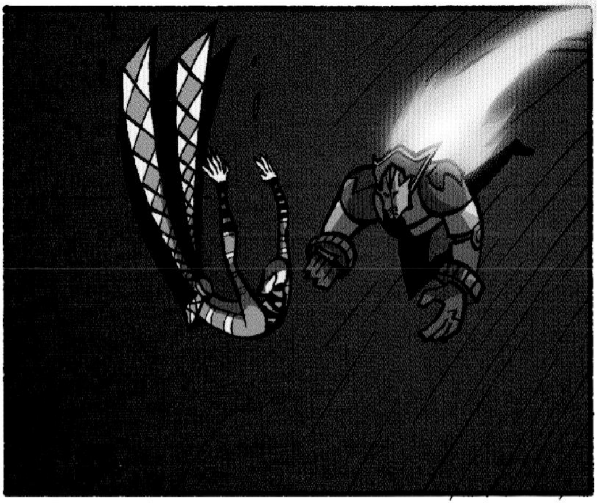
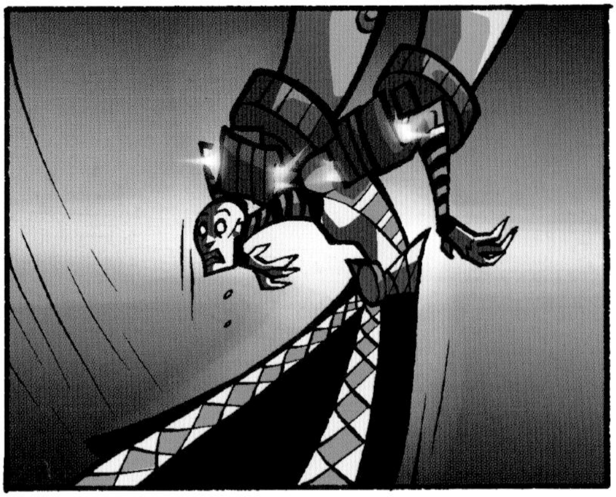
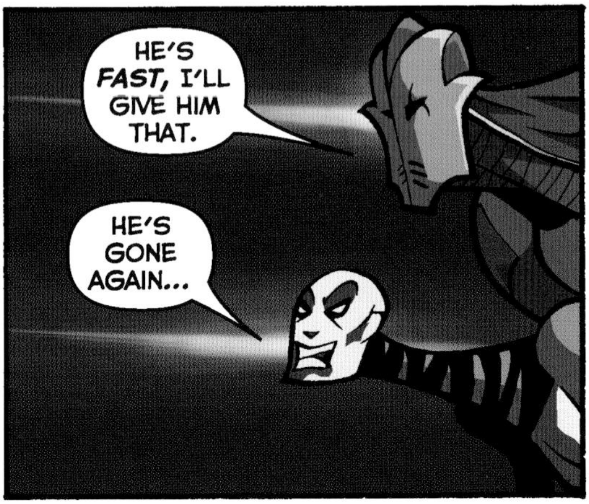
HE'S *FAST,* I'LL GIVE HIM THAT.
HE'S GONE AGAIN...

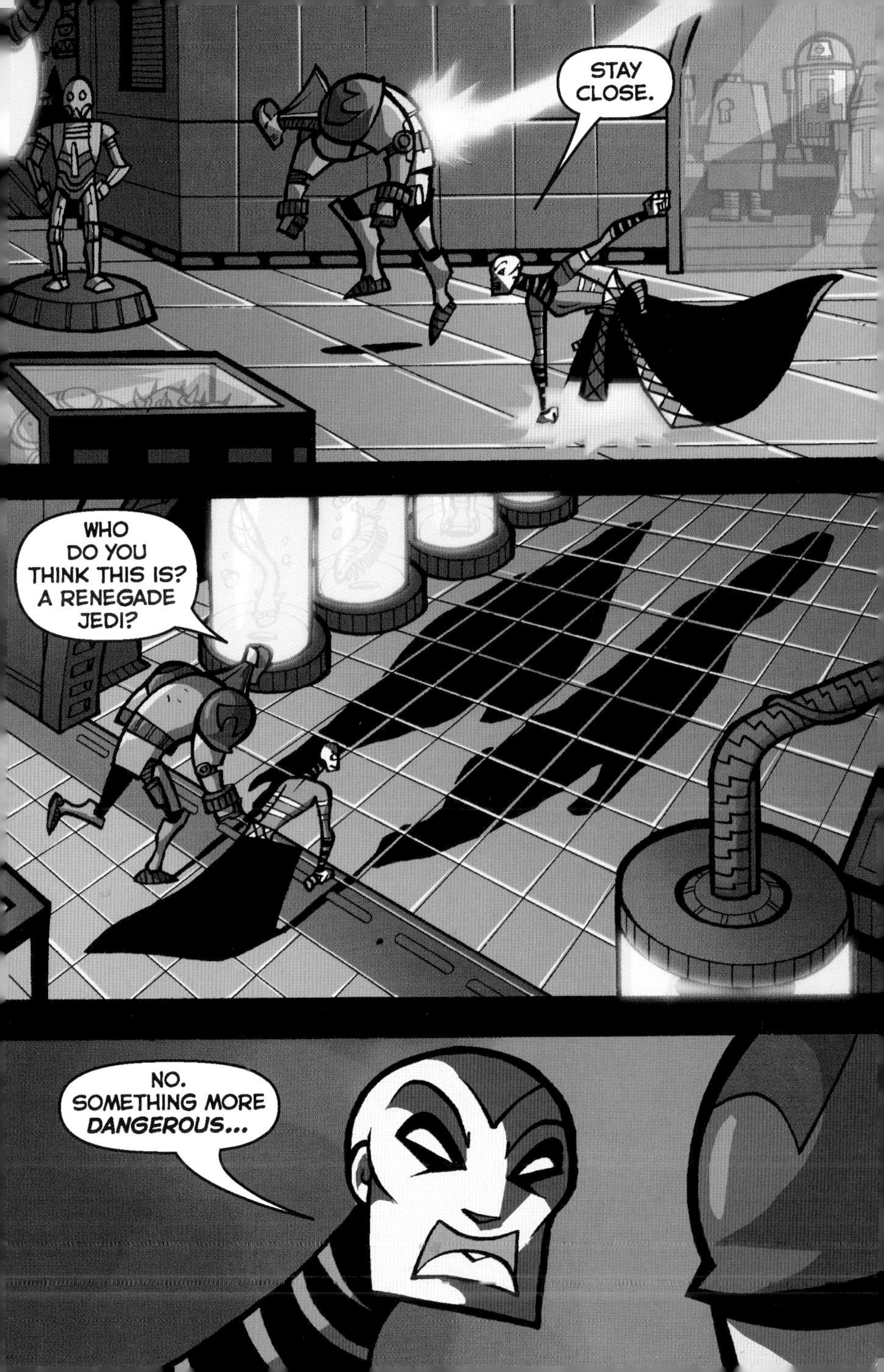
STAY CLOSE.
WHO DO YOU THINK THIS IS? A RENEGADE JEDI?
NO. SOMETHING MORE *DANGEROUS...*

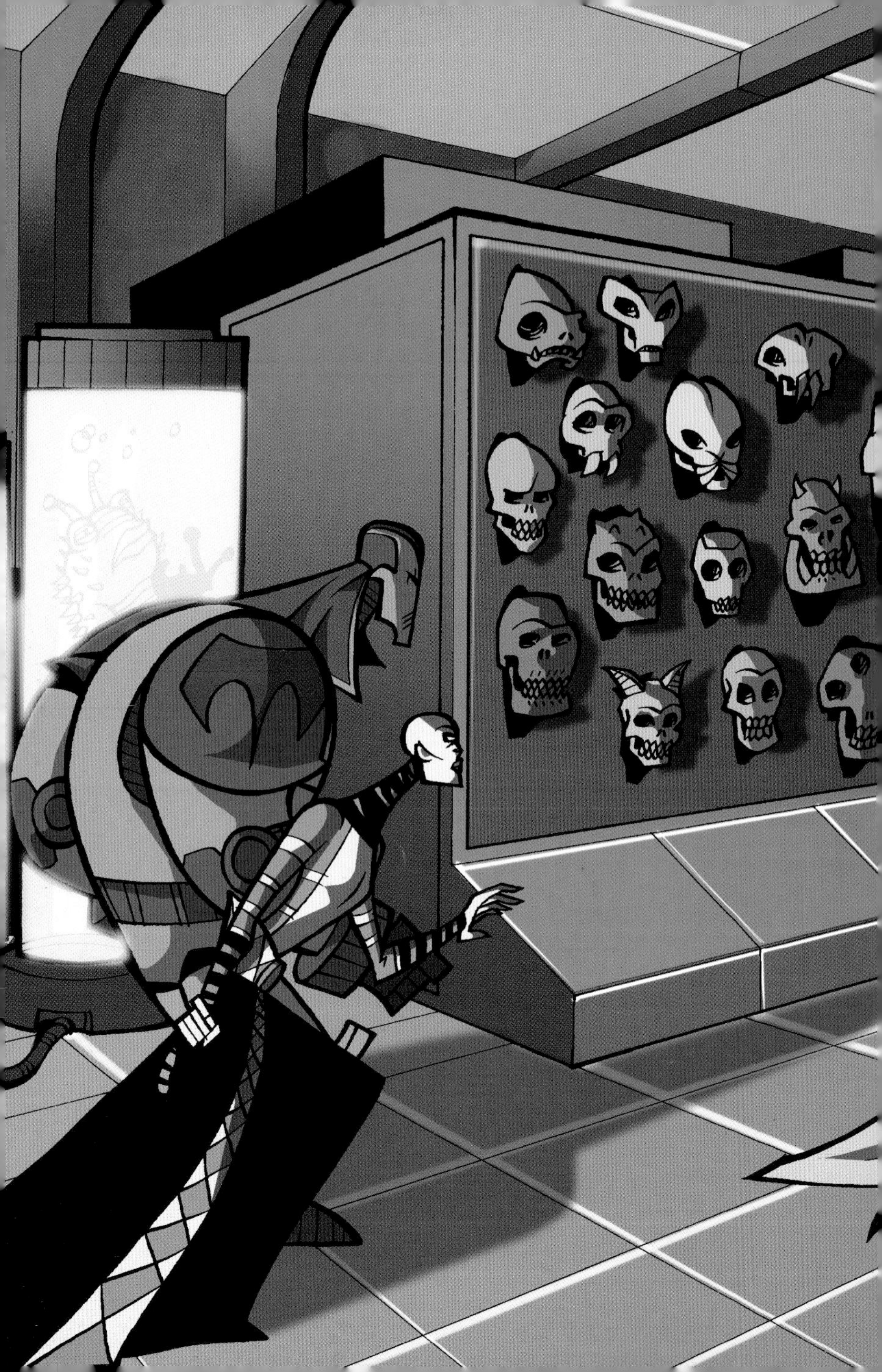

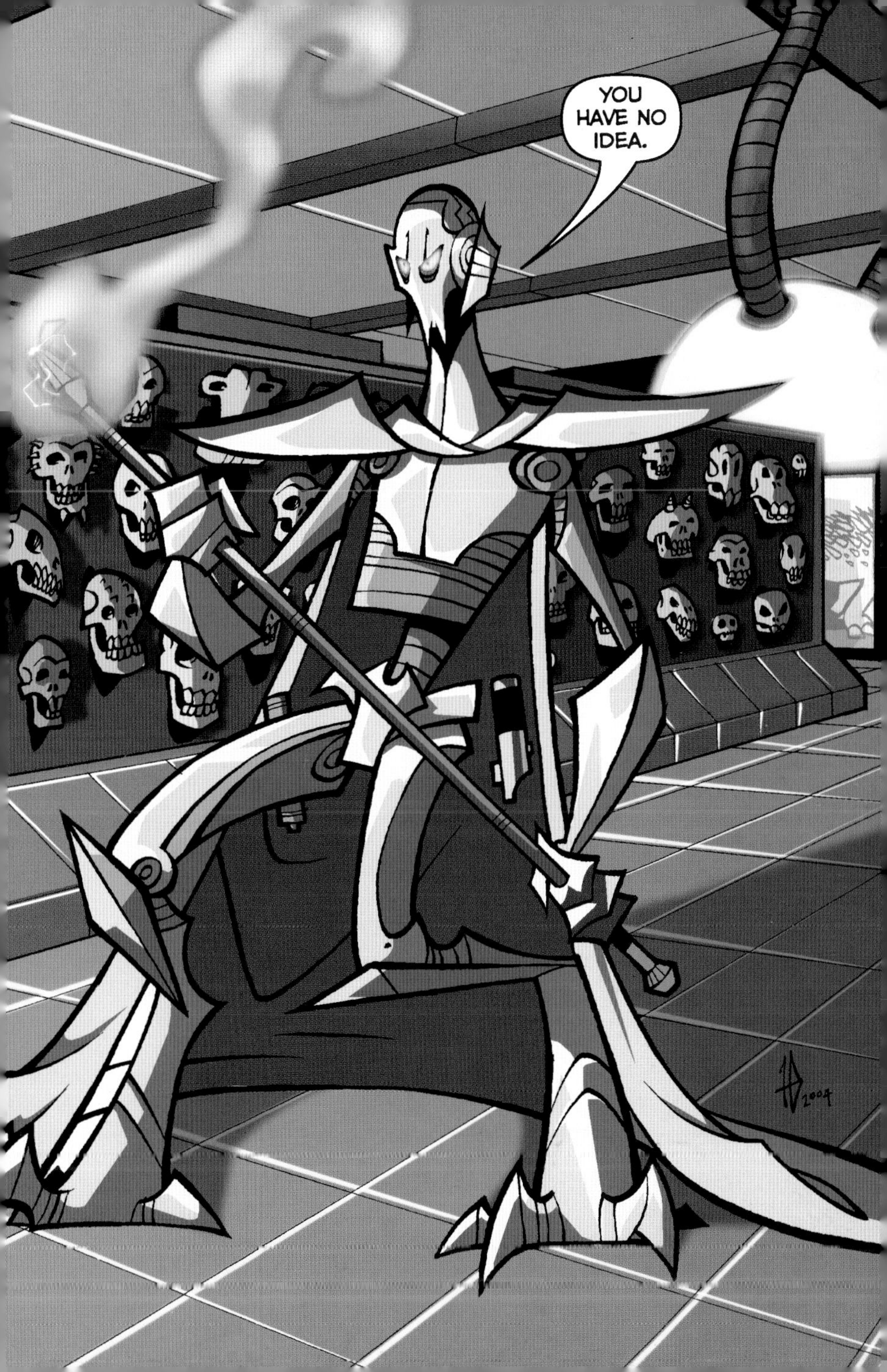
YOU HAVE NO IDEA.

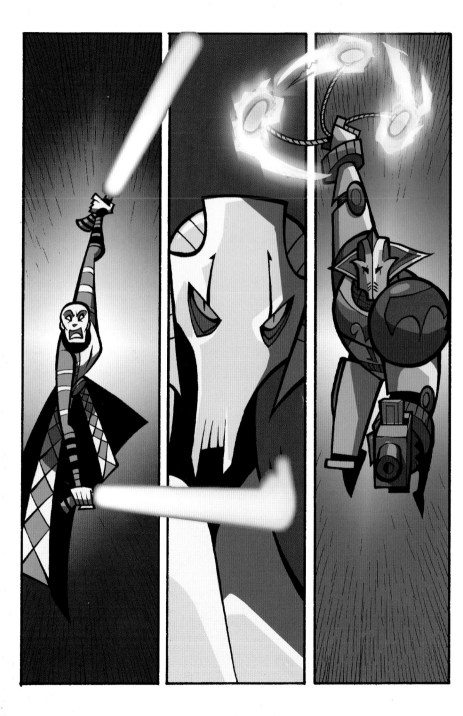

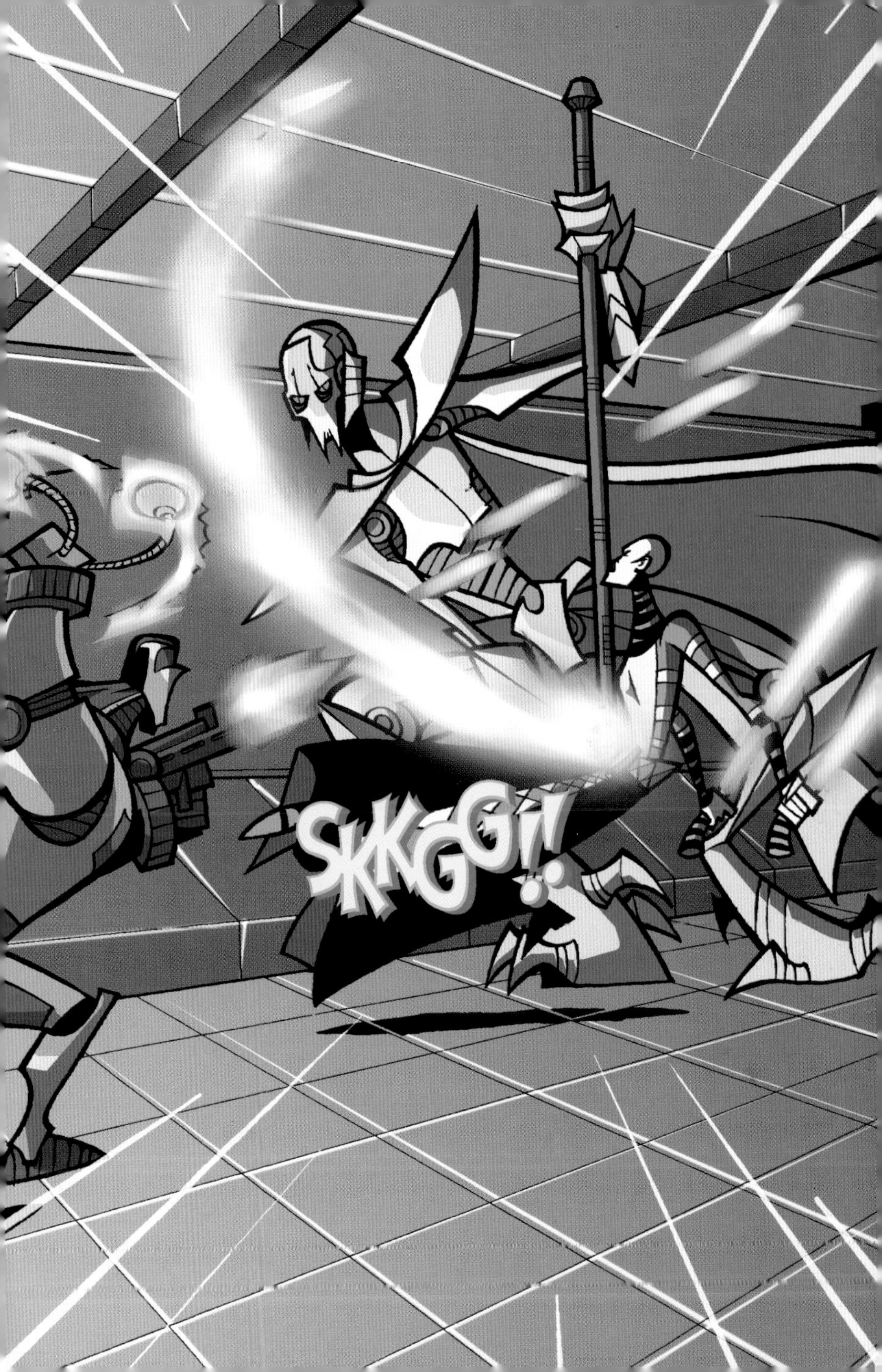
SKKGG!!

KRISH!

ZZZAAPP!

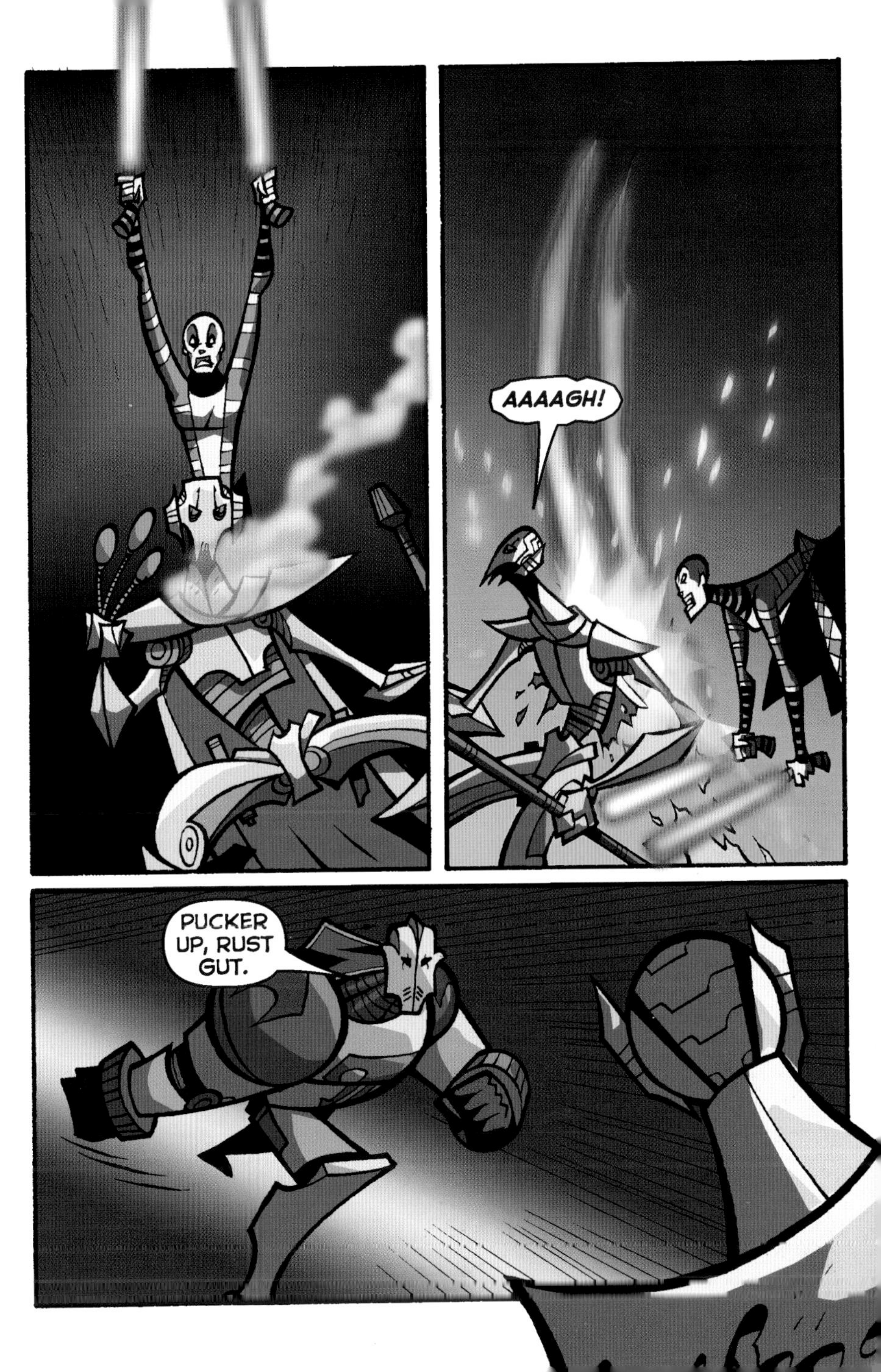
AAAAGH!
PUCKER UP, RUST GUT.

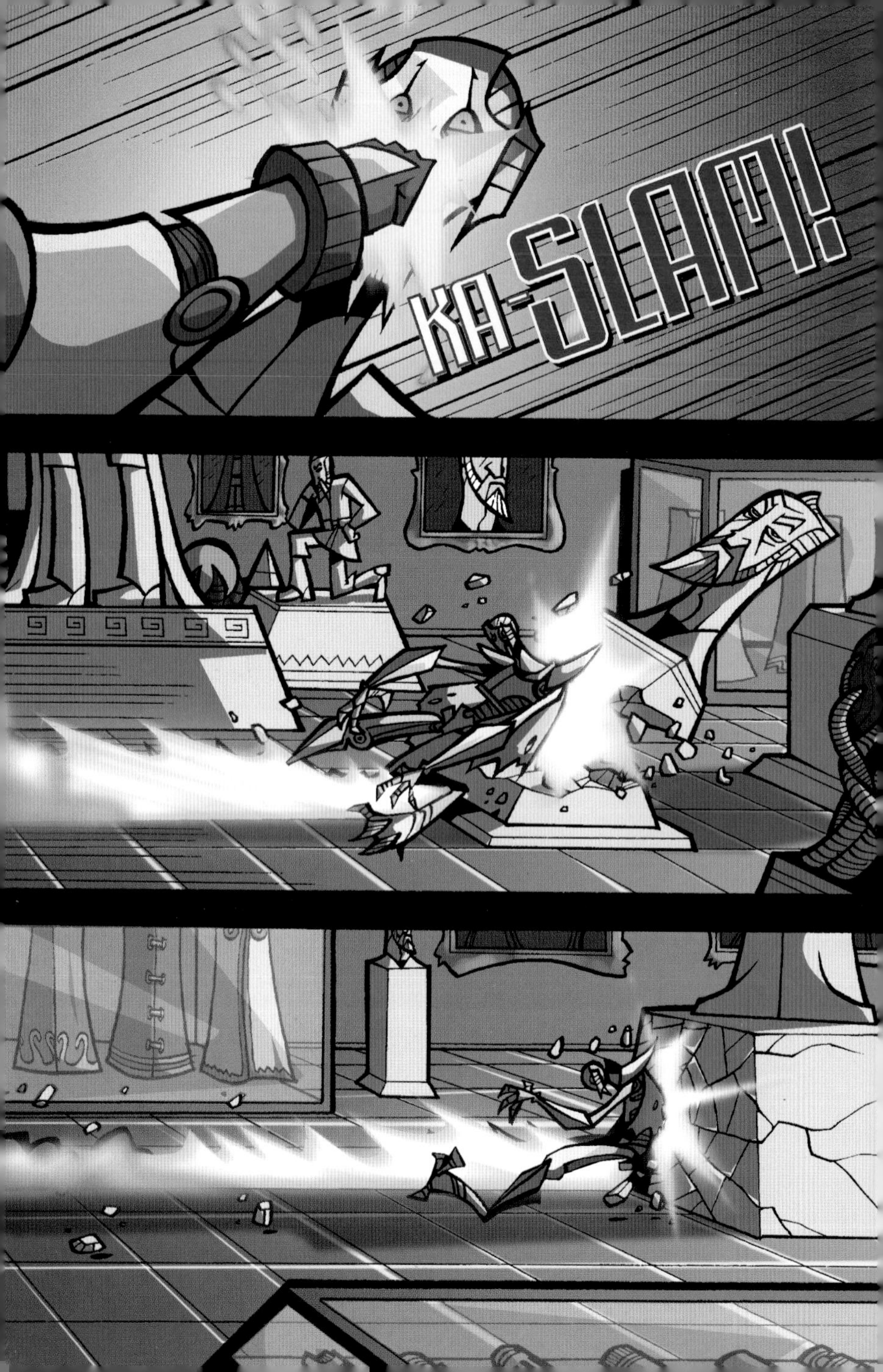
KA-SLAM!

KLICK!

WHIRR!

VWMM!

VVMMM!

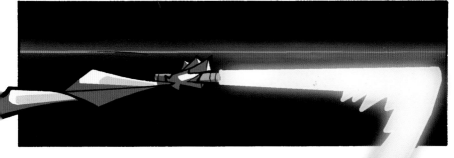

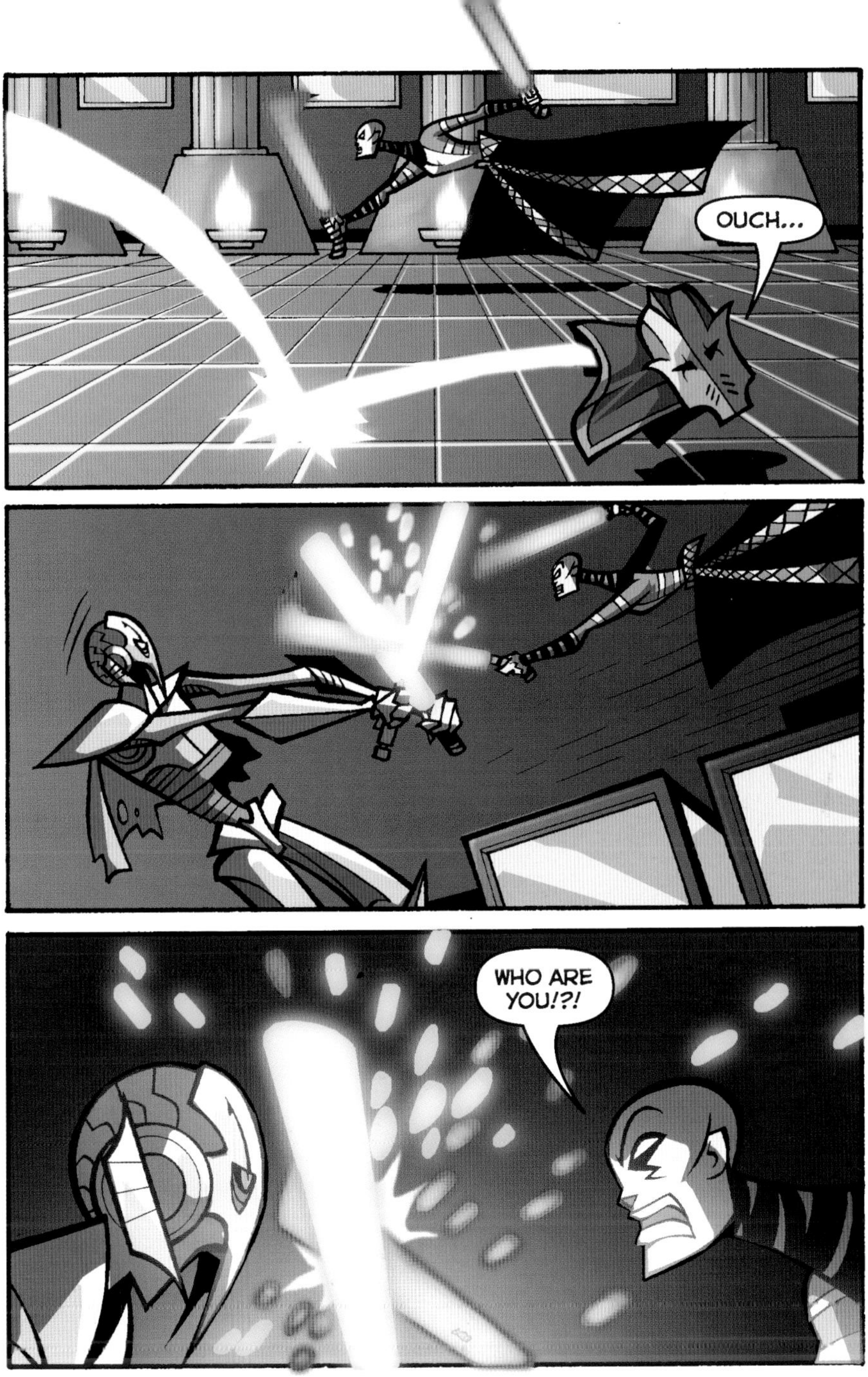
OUCH...
WHO ARE YOU!?!

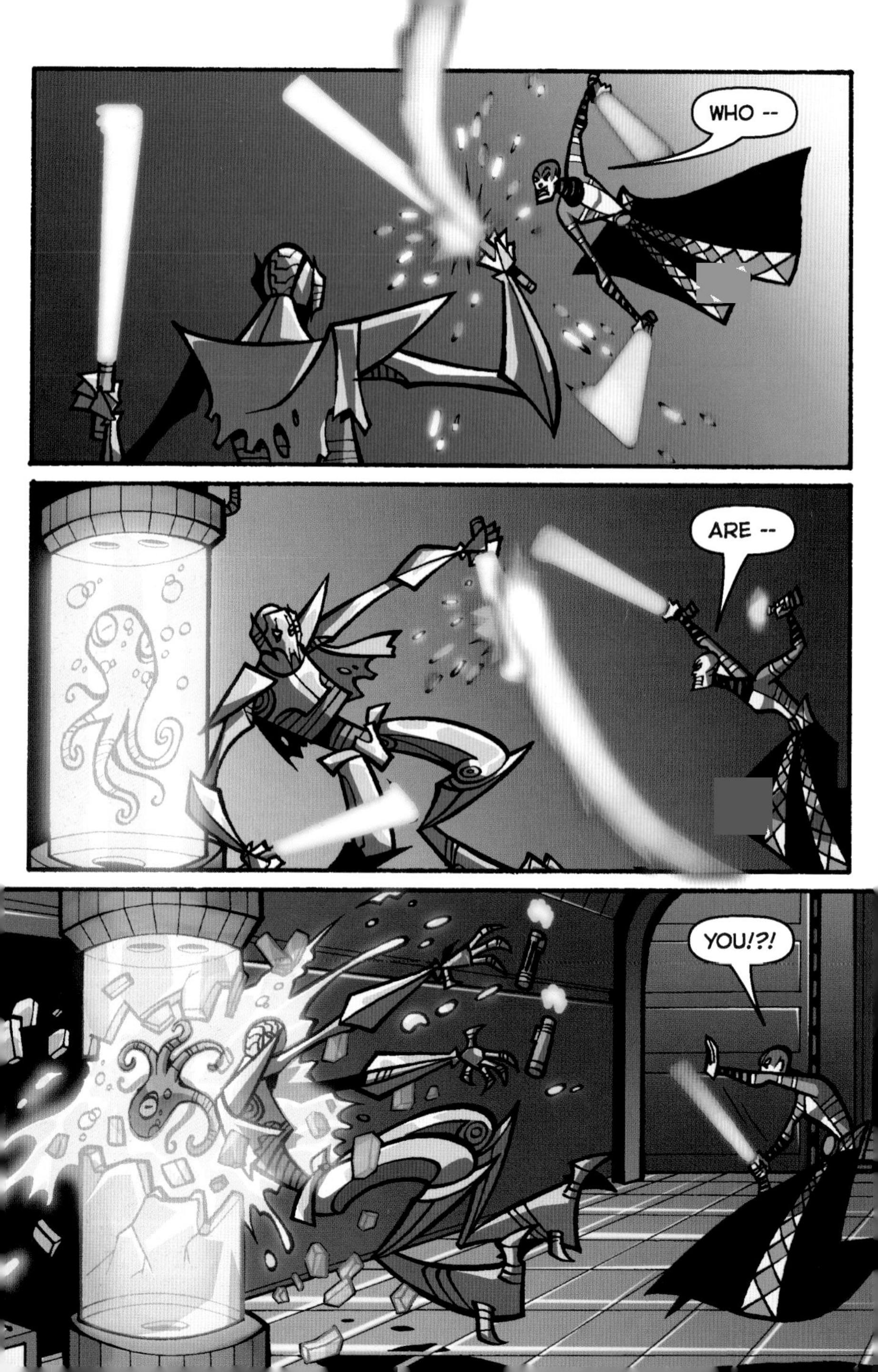
WHO --
ARE --
YOU!?!

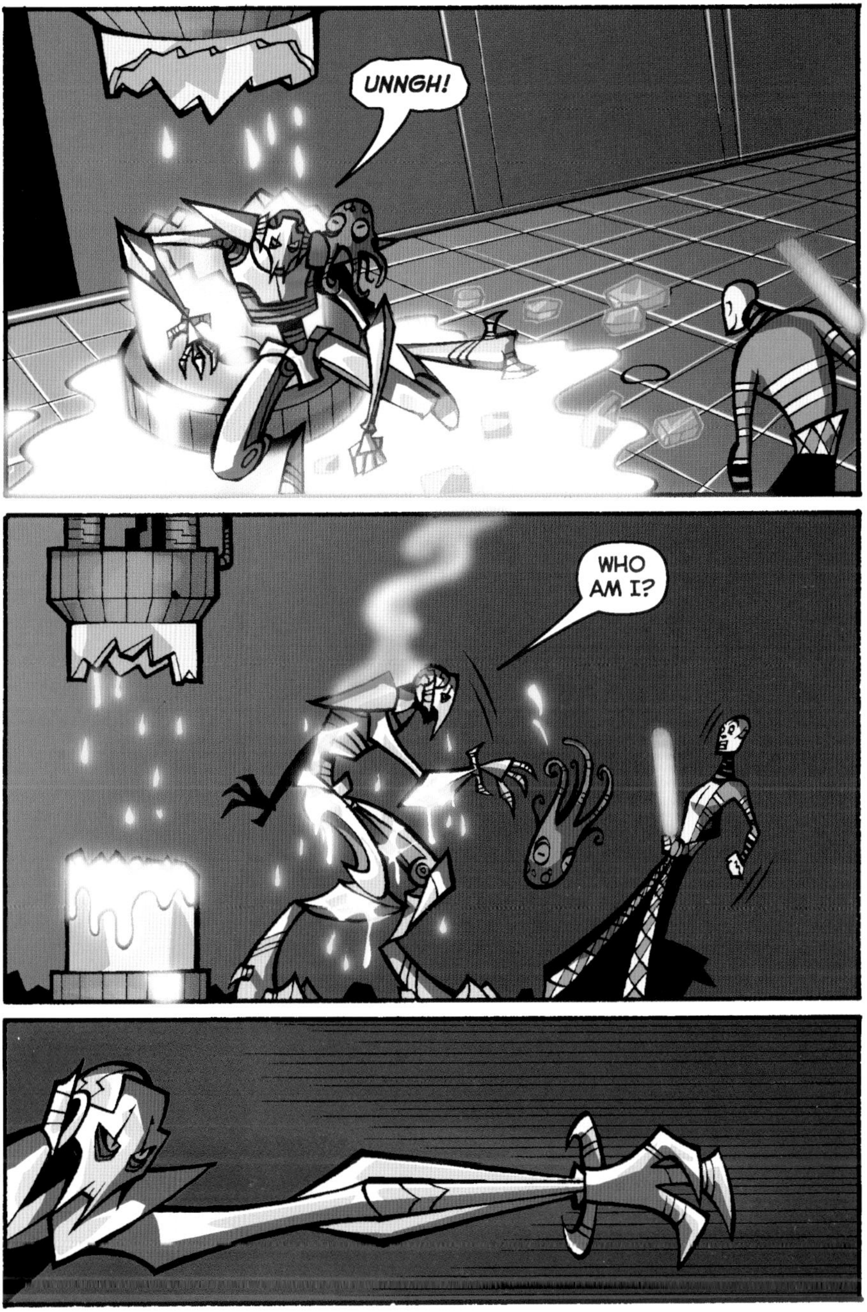
UNNGH!
WHO AM I?

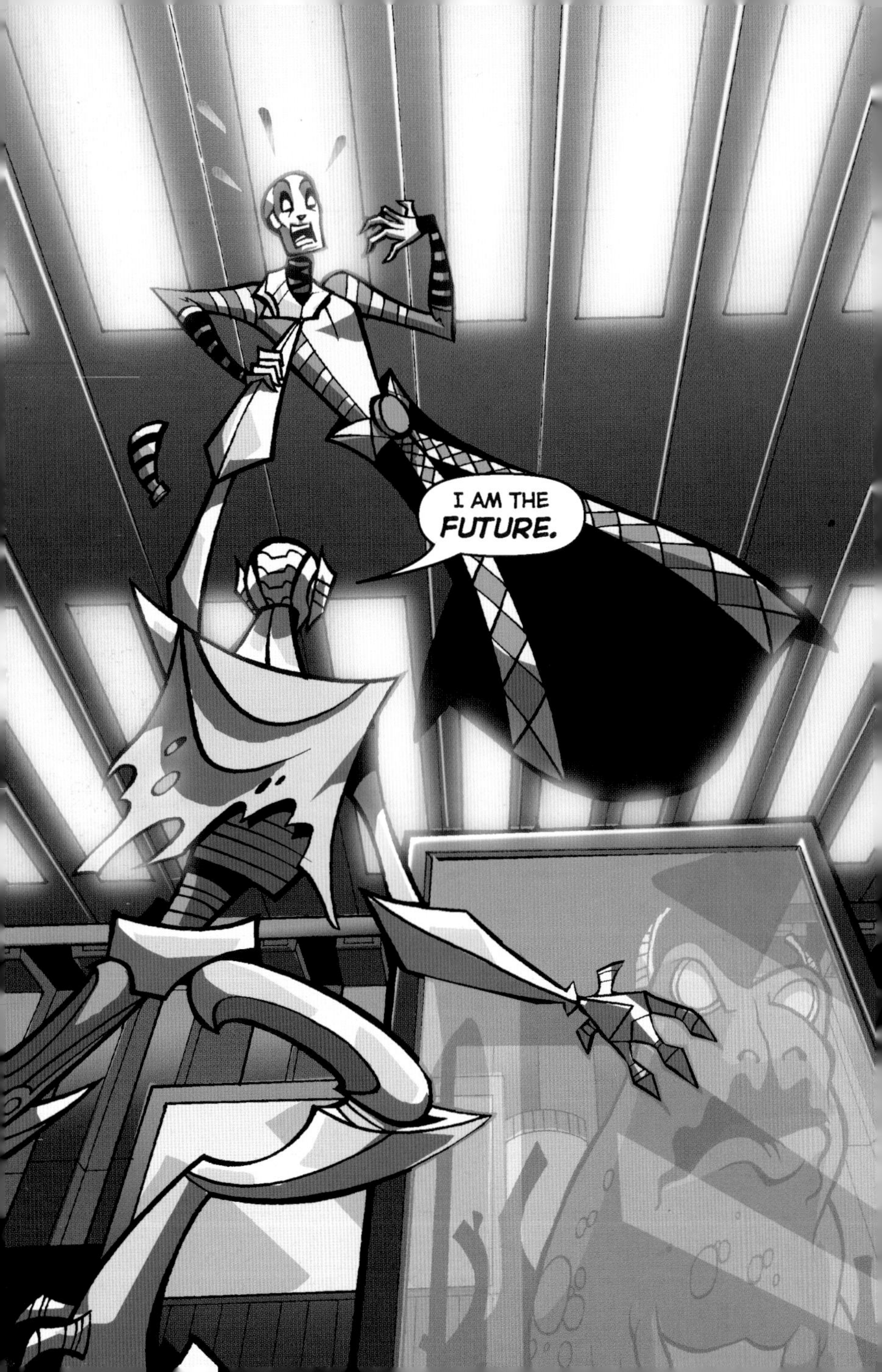
I AM THE FUTURE.

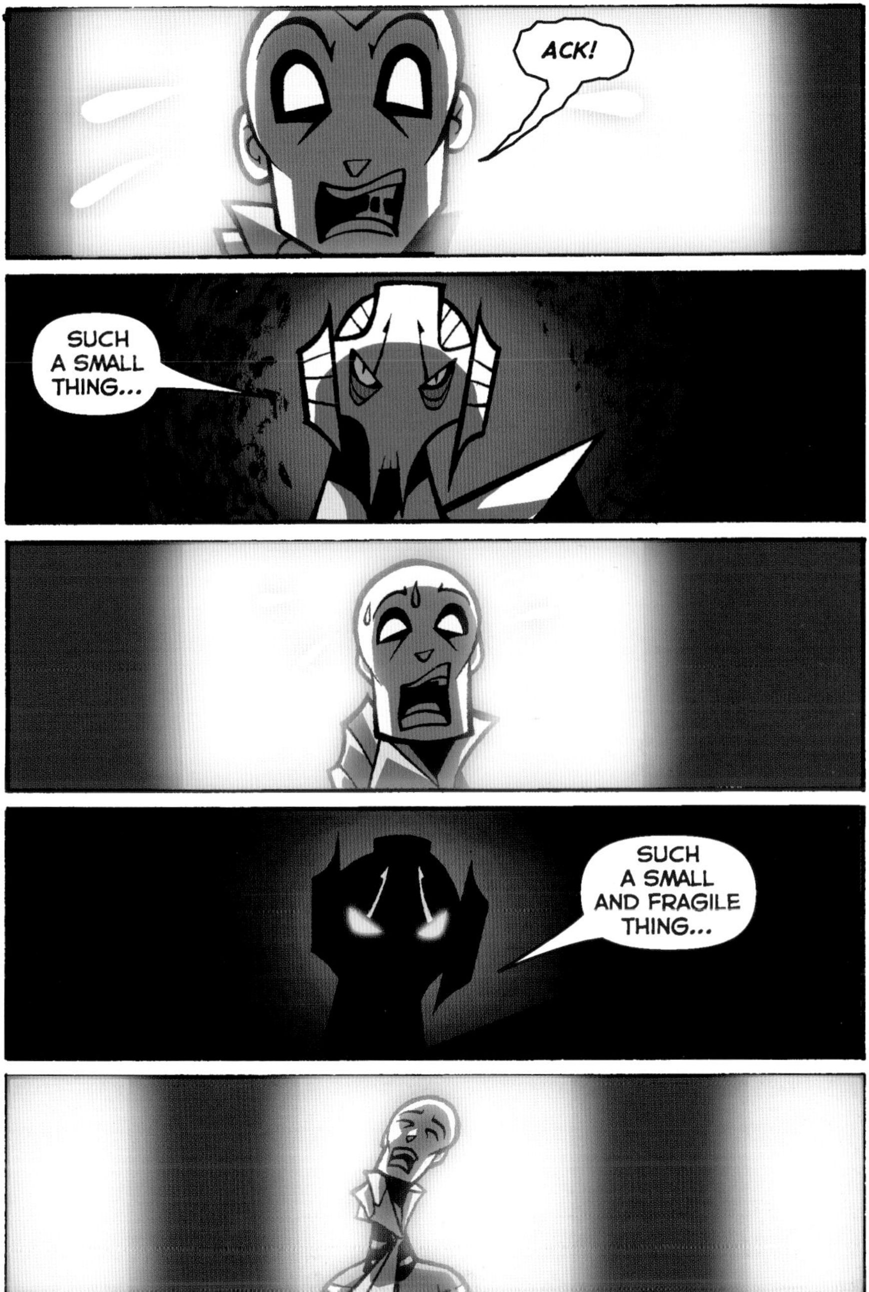
ACK!
SUCH A SMALL THING...
SUCH A SMALL AND FRAGILE THING...

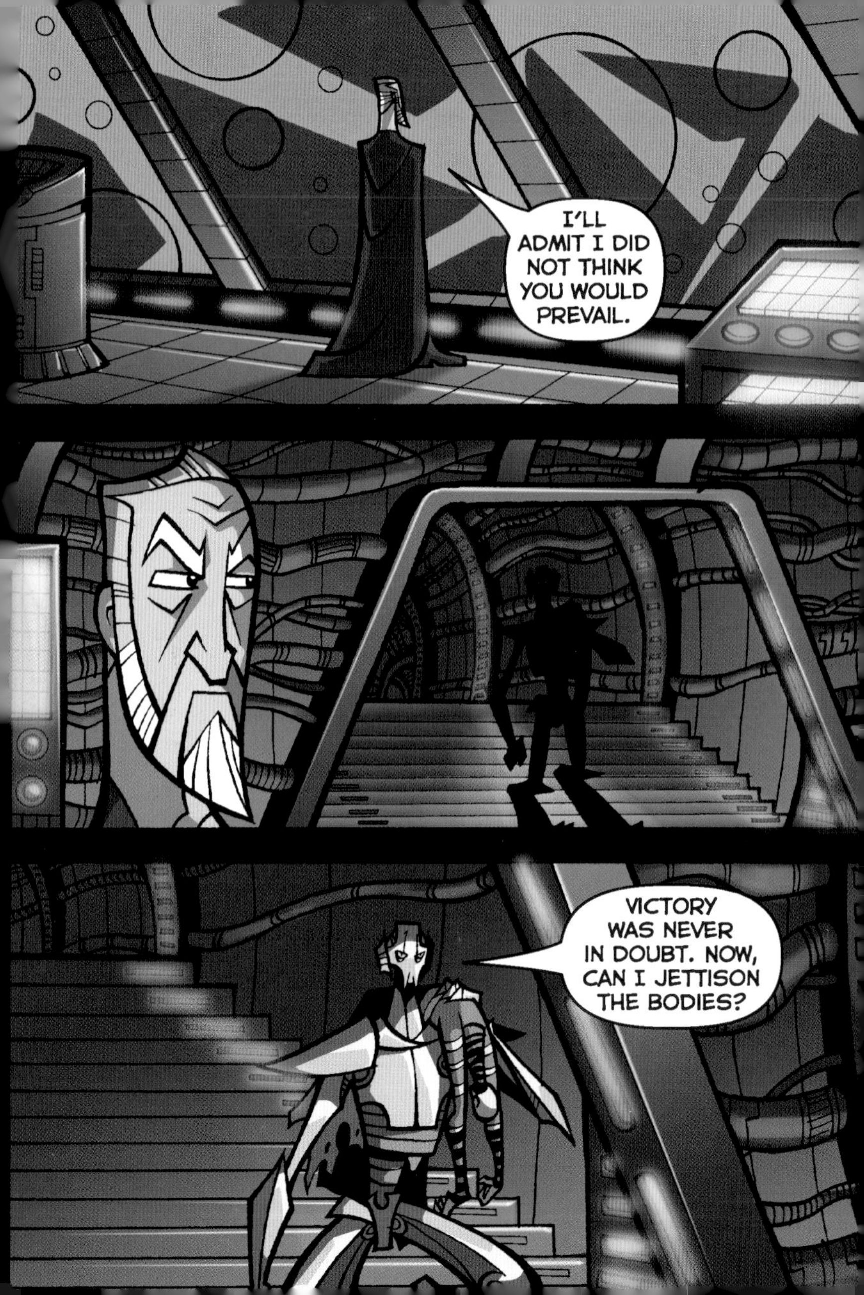
I'LL ADMIT I DID NOT THINK YOU WOULD PREVAIL.
VICTORY WAS NEVER IN DOUBT. NOW, CAN I JETTISON THE BODIES?

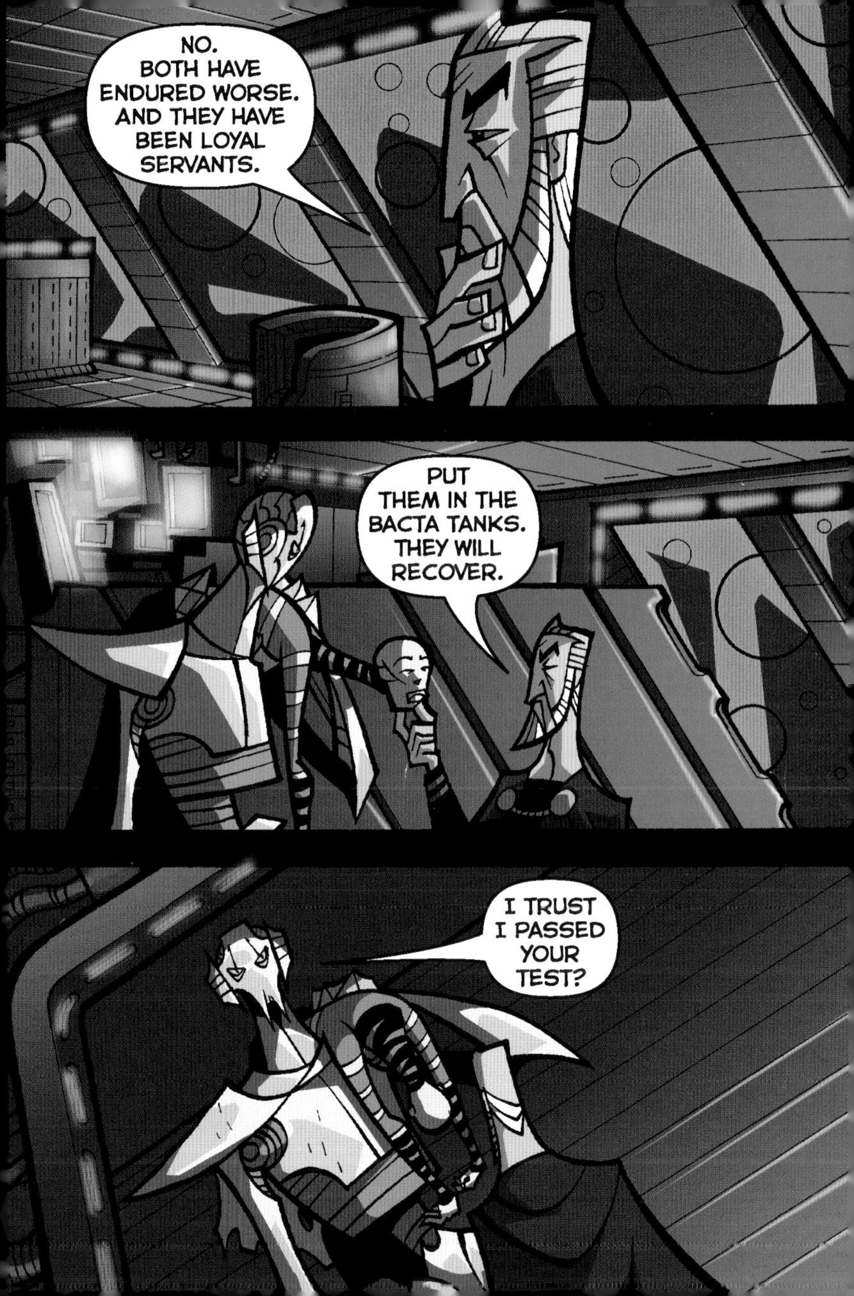
NO. BOTH HAVE ENDURED WORSE. AND THEY HAVE BEEN LOYAL SERVANTS.
PUT THEM IN THE BACTA TANKS. THEY WILL RECOVER.
I TRUST I PASSED YOUR TEST?

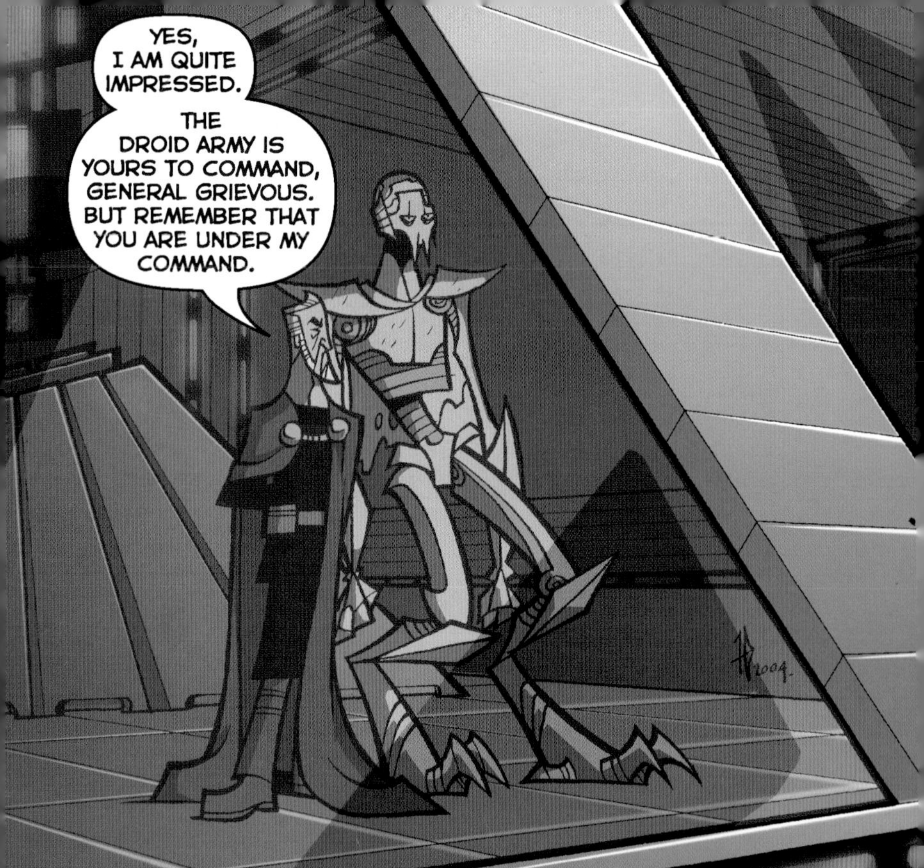
YES, I AM QUITE IMPRESSED.
THE DROID ARMY IS YOURS TO COMMAND, GENERAL GRIEVOUS. BUT REMEMBER THAT YOU ARE UNDER MY COMMAND.

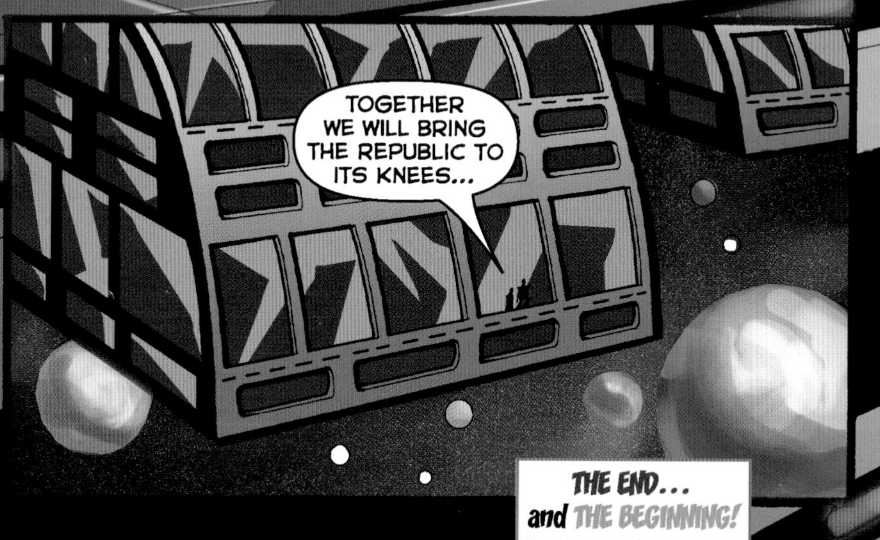
TOGETHER WE WILL BRING THE REPUBLIC TO ITS KNEES...
THE END... and THE BEGINNING!

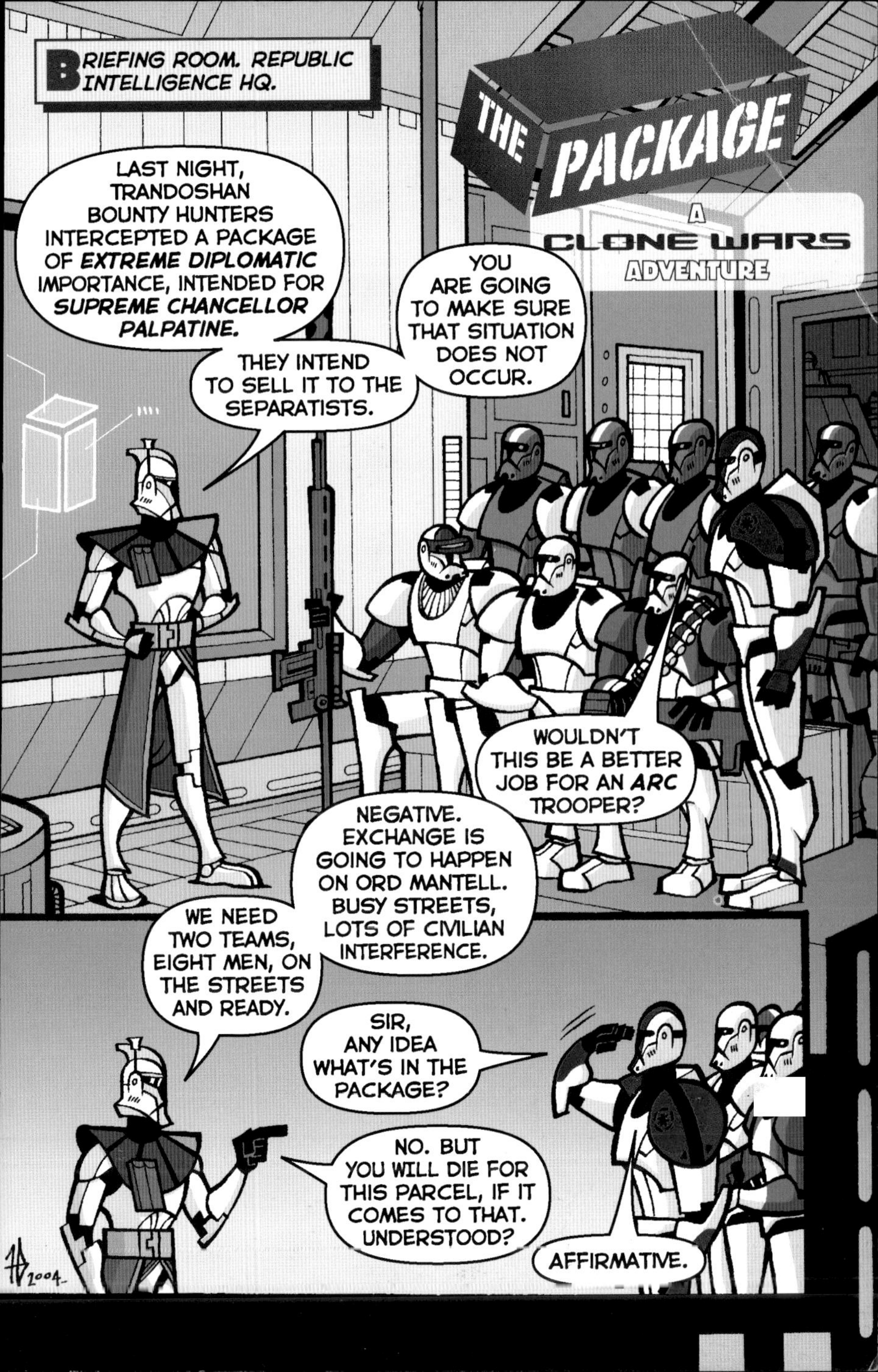
BRIEFING ROOM. REPUBLIC INTELLIGENCE HQ.
THE PACKAGE
A CLONE WARS ADVENTURE
LAST NIGHT, TRANDOSHAN BOUNTY HUNTERS INTERCEPTED A PACKAGE OF EXTREME DIPLOMATIC IMPORTANCE, INTENDED FOR SUPREME CHANCELLOR PALPATINE.
THEY INTEND TO SELL IT TO THE SEPARATISTS.
YOU ARE GOING TO MAKE SURE THAT SITUATION DOES NOT OCCUR.
WOULDN'T THIS BE A BETTER JOB FOR AN ARC TROOPER?
NEGATIVE. EXCHANGE IS GOING TO HAPPEN ON ORD MANTELL. BUSY STREETS, LOTS OF CIVILIAN INTERFERENCE.
WE NEED TWO TEAMS, EIGHT MEN, ON THE STREETS AND READY.
SIR, ANY IDEA WHAT'S IN THE PACKAGE?
NO. BUT YOU WILL DIE FOR THIS PARCEL, IF IT COMES TO THAT. UNDERSTOOD?
AFFIRMATIVE.
2004

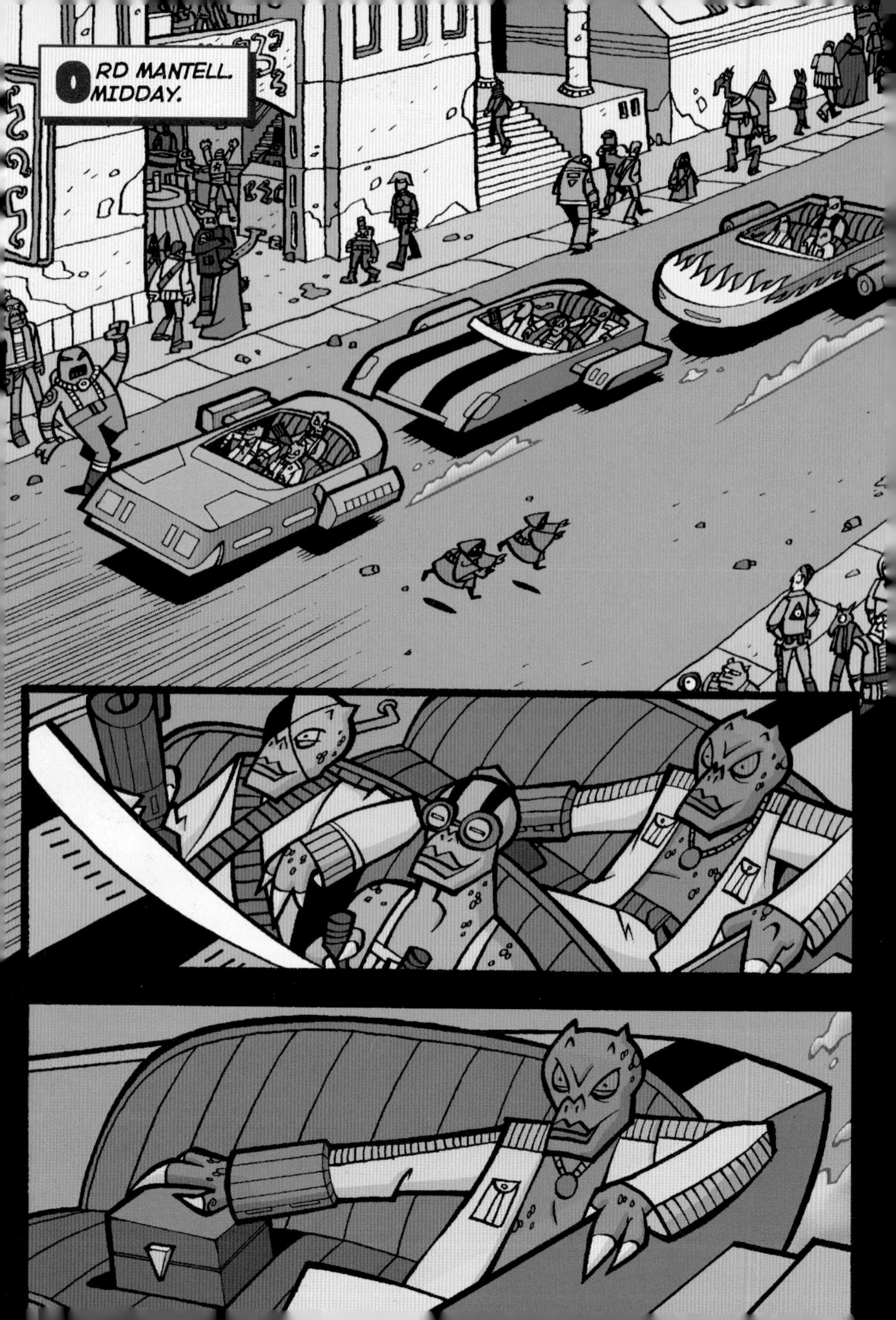
ORD MANTELL.
MIDDAY.

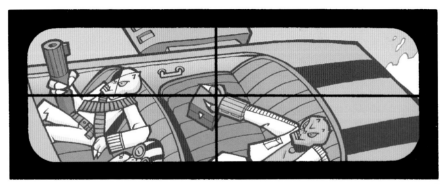

I SEE THE PACKAGE. SECOND SPEEDER.

GOOD. NOW WE THIN THE RANKS.

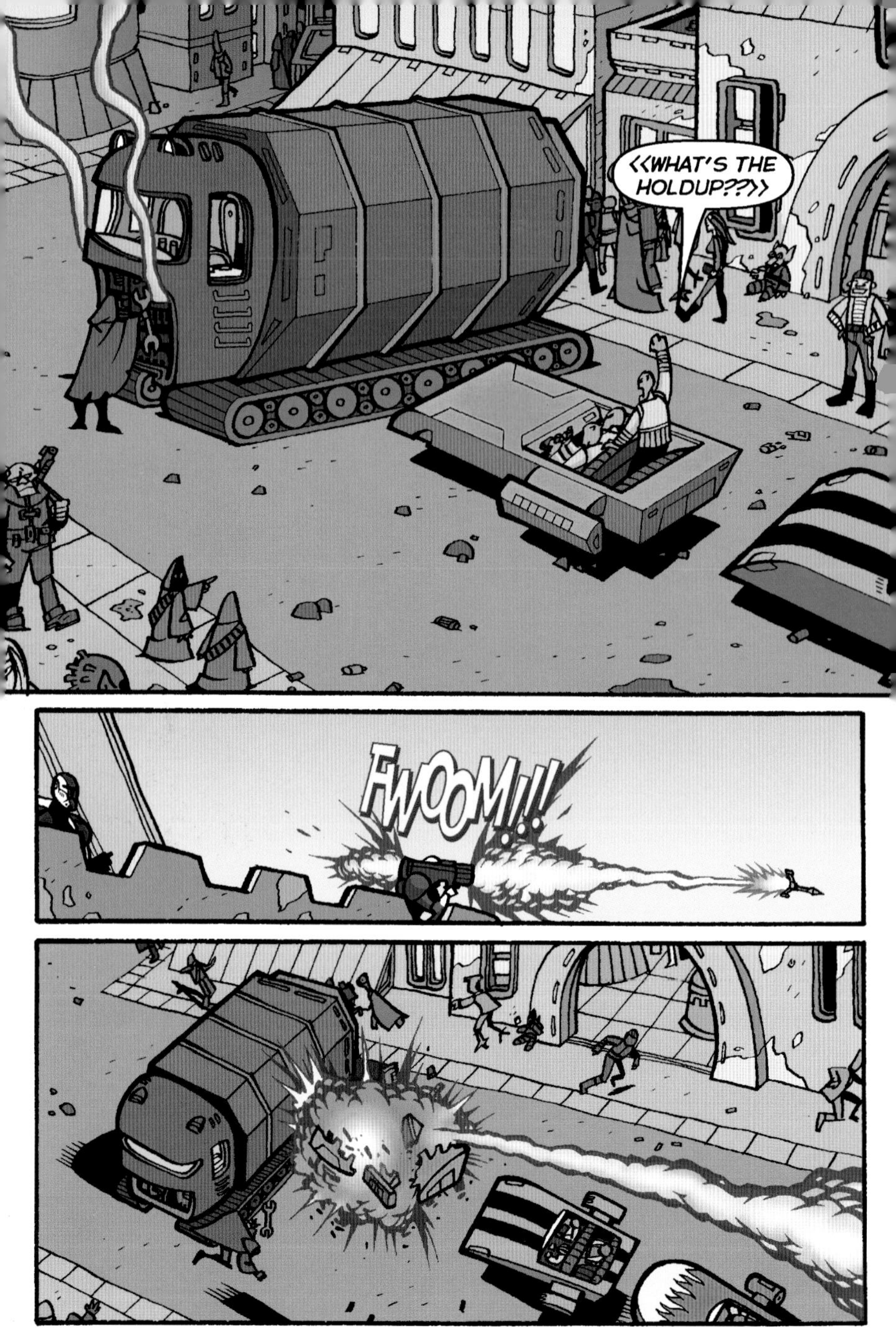
<<WHAT'S THE HOLDUP??>>
FWOOM!!!

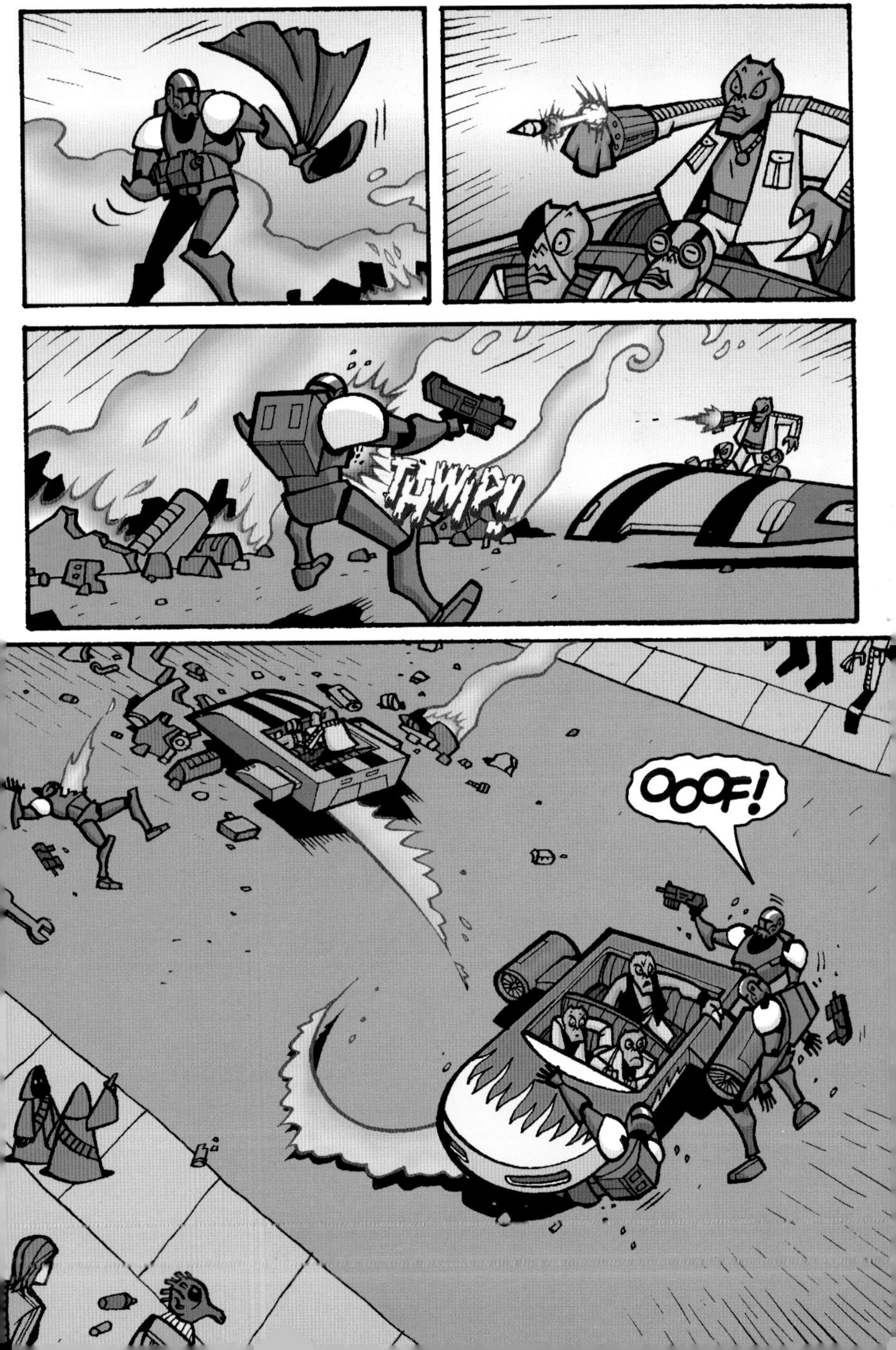
THWIP!
OOOF!

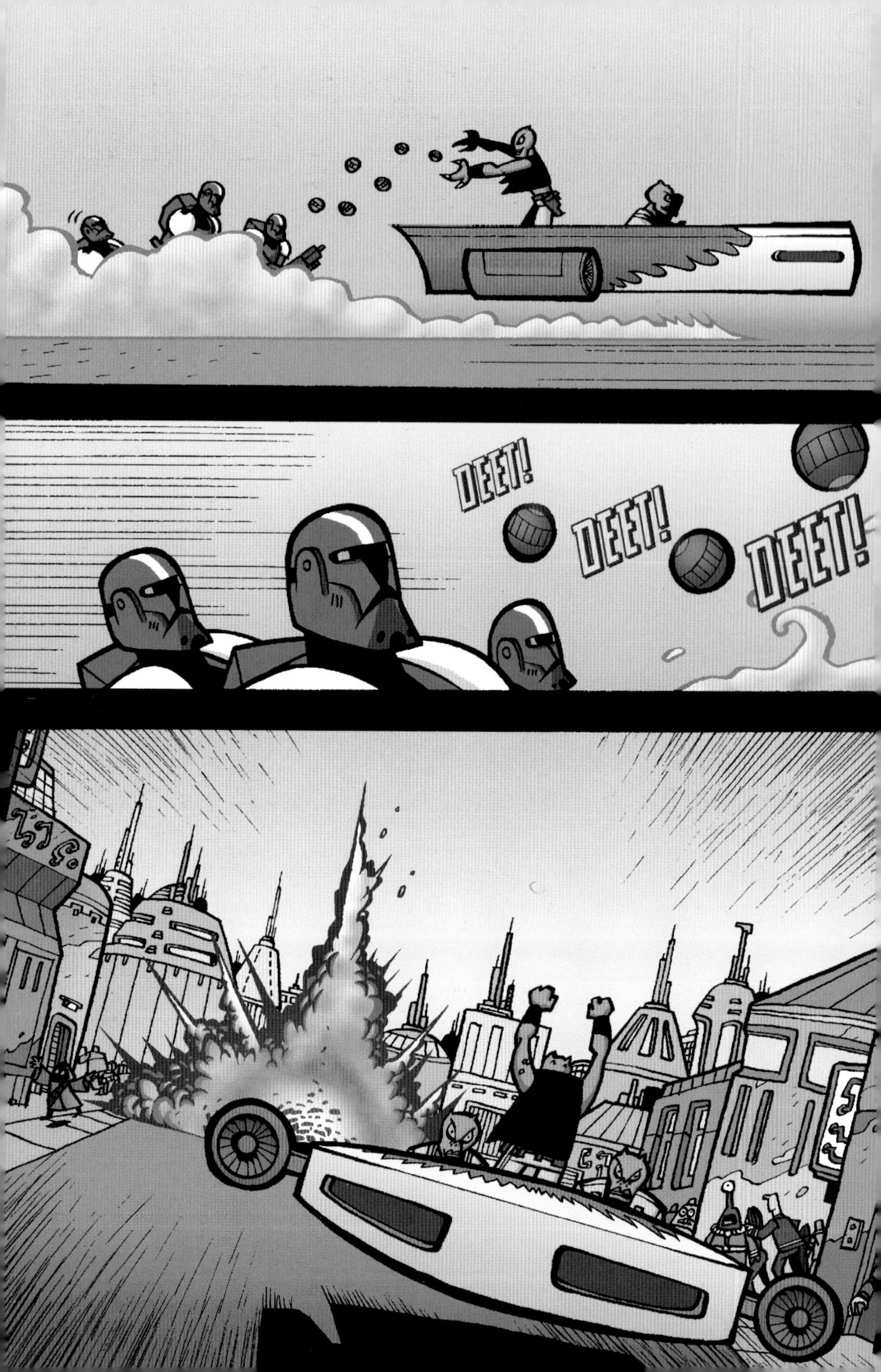
DEET!
DEET!
DEET!

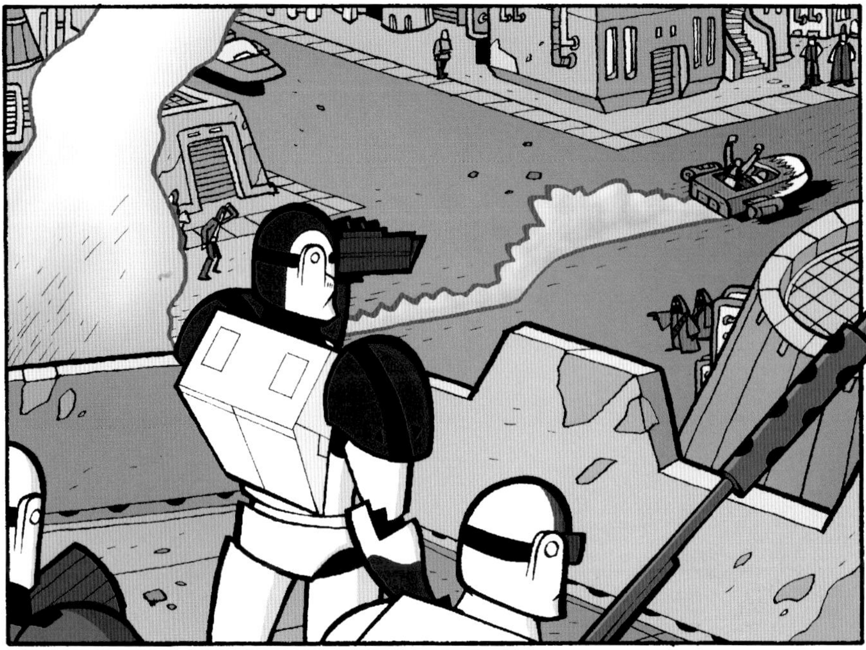

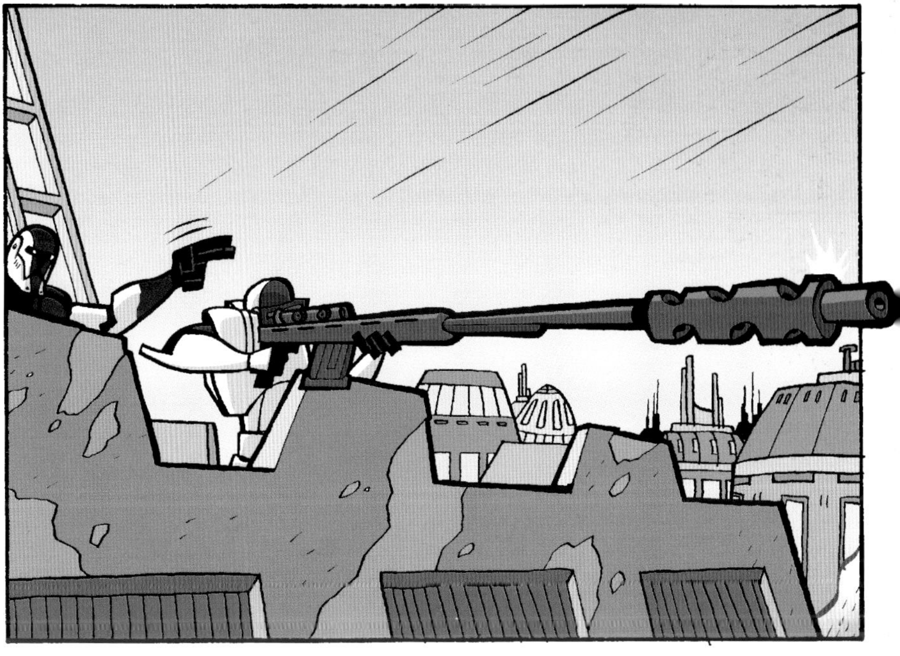

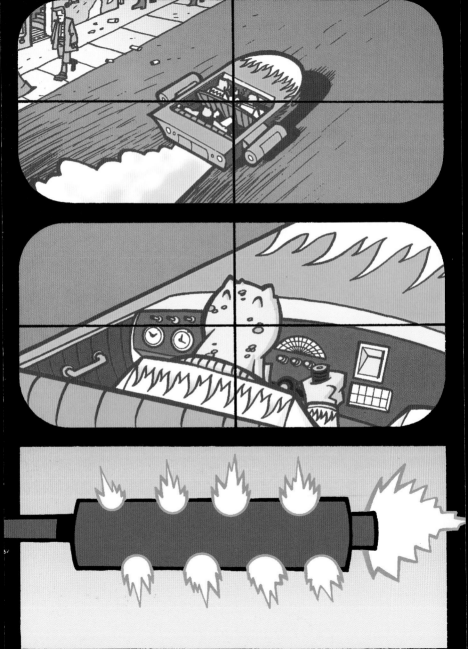

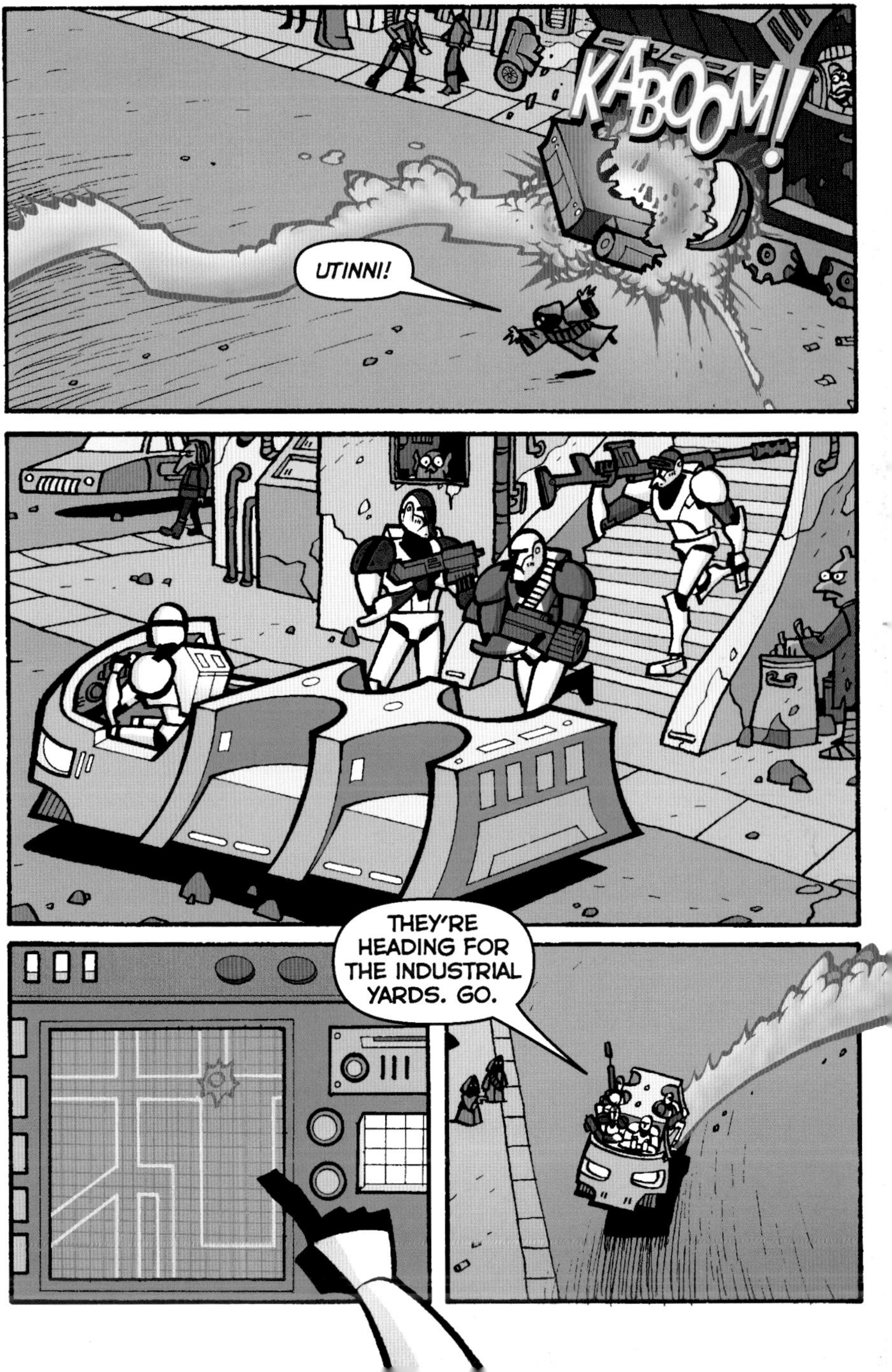
KABOOM!
UTINNI!
THEY'RE HEADING FOR THE INDUSTRIAL YARDS. GO.

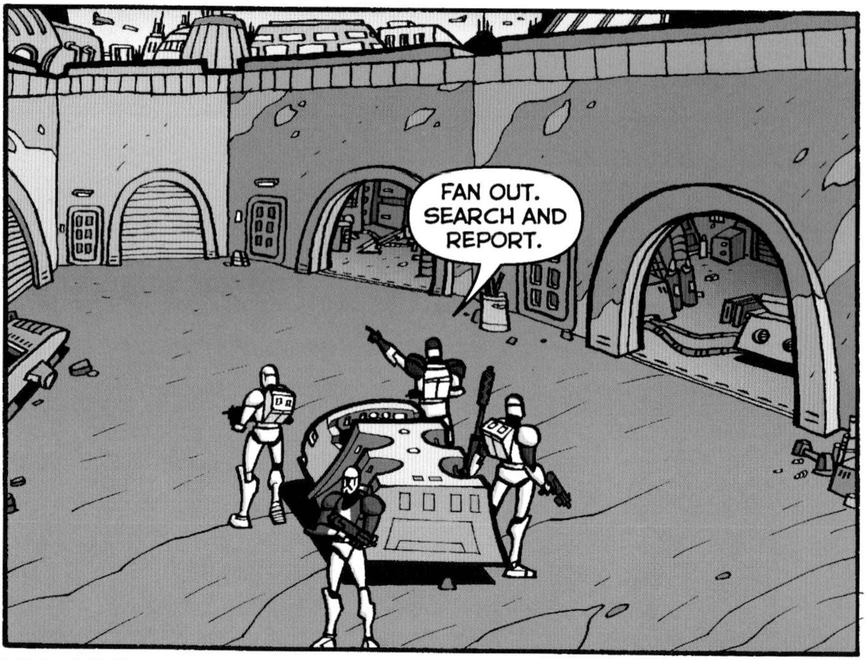
FAN OUT. SEARCH AND REPORT.

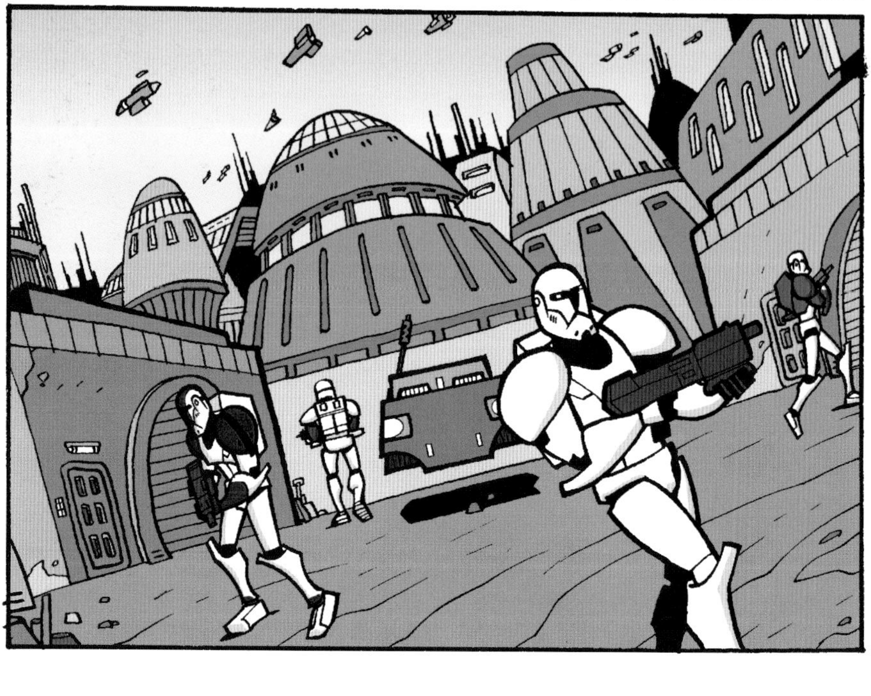

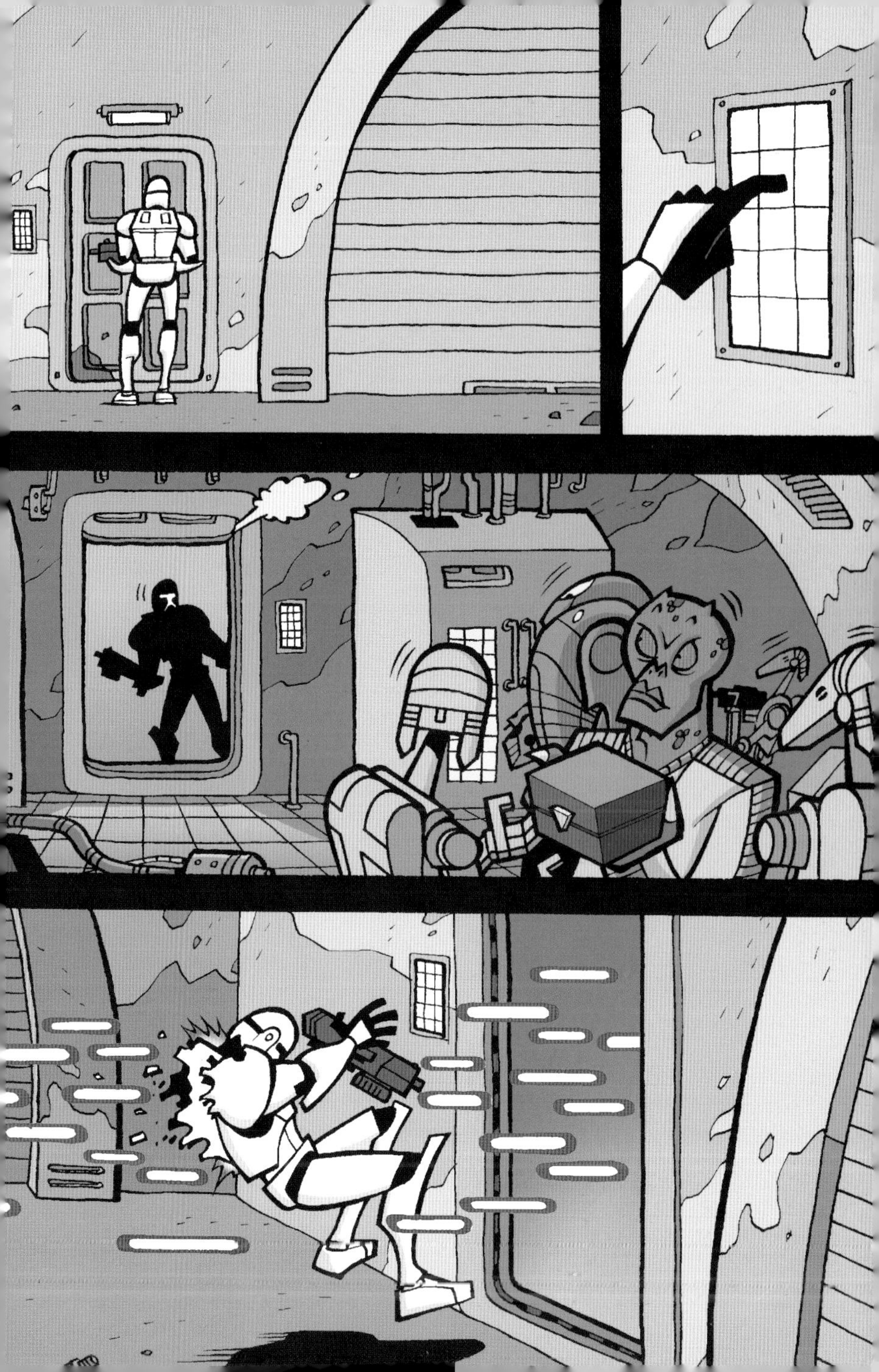

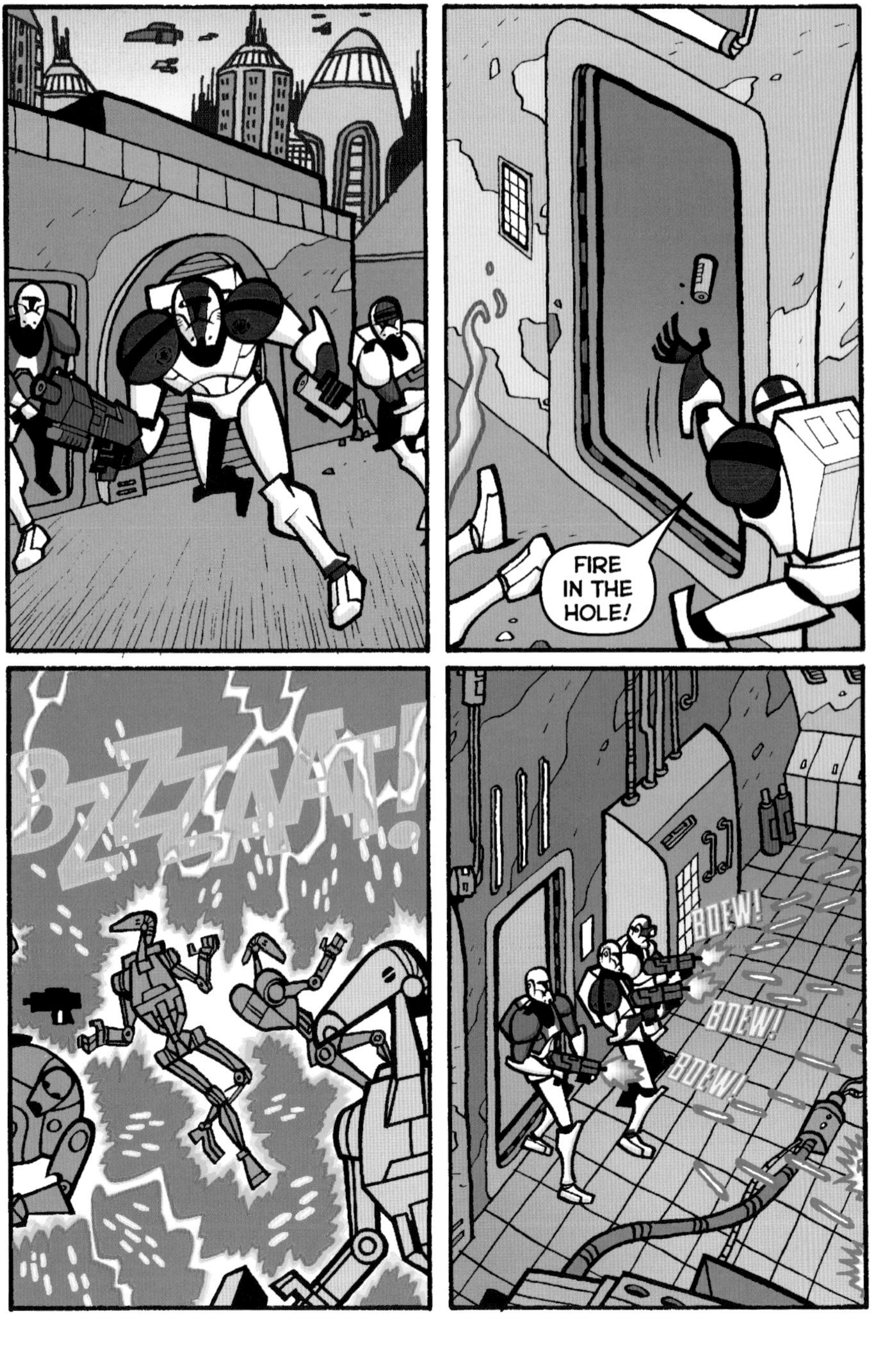
FIRE IN THE HOLE!
BZZAAT!
BOEW!
BOEW!
BOEW!

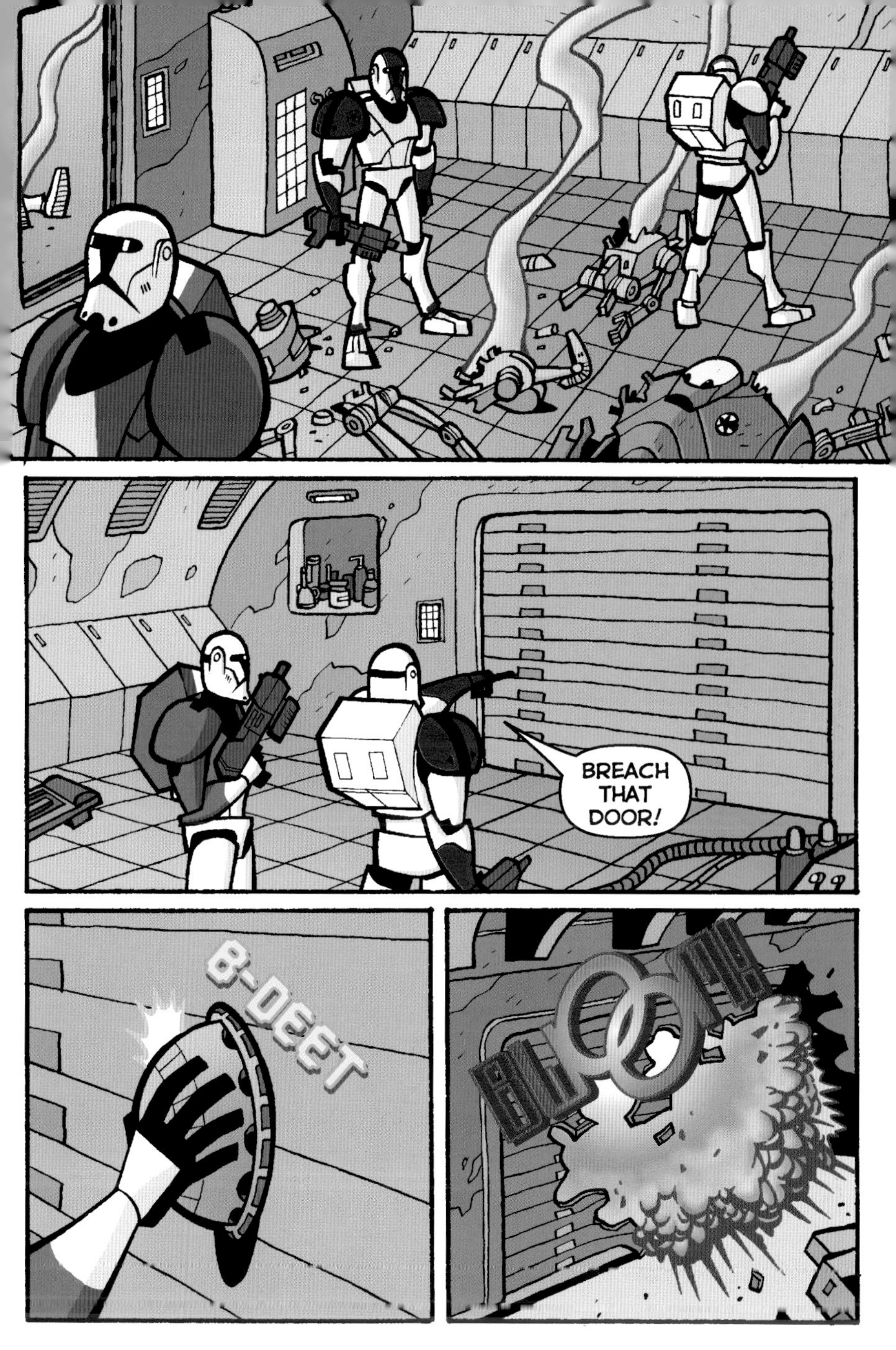
BREACH THAT DOOR!
B-DEET
BOOM!

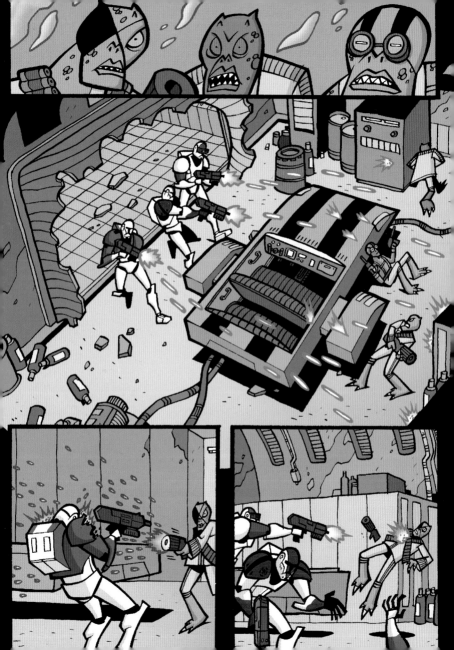

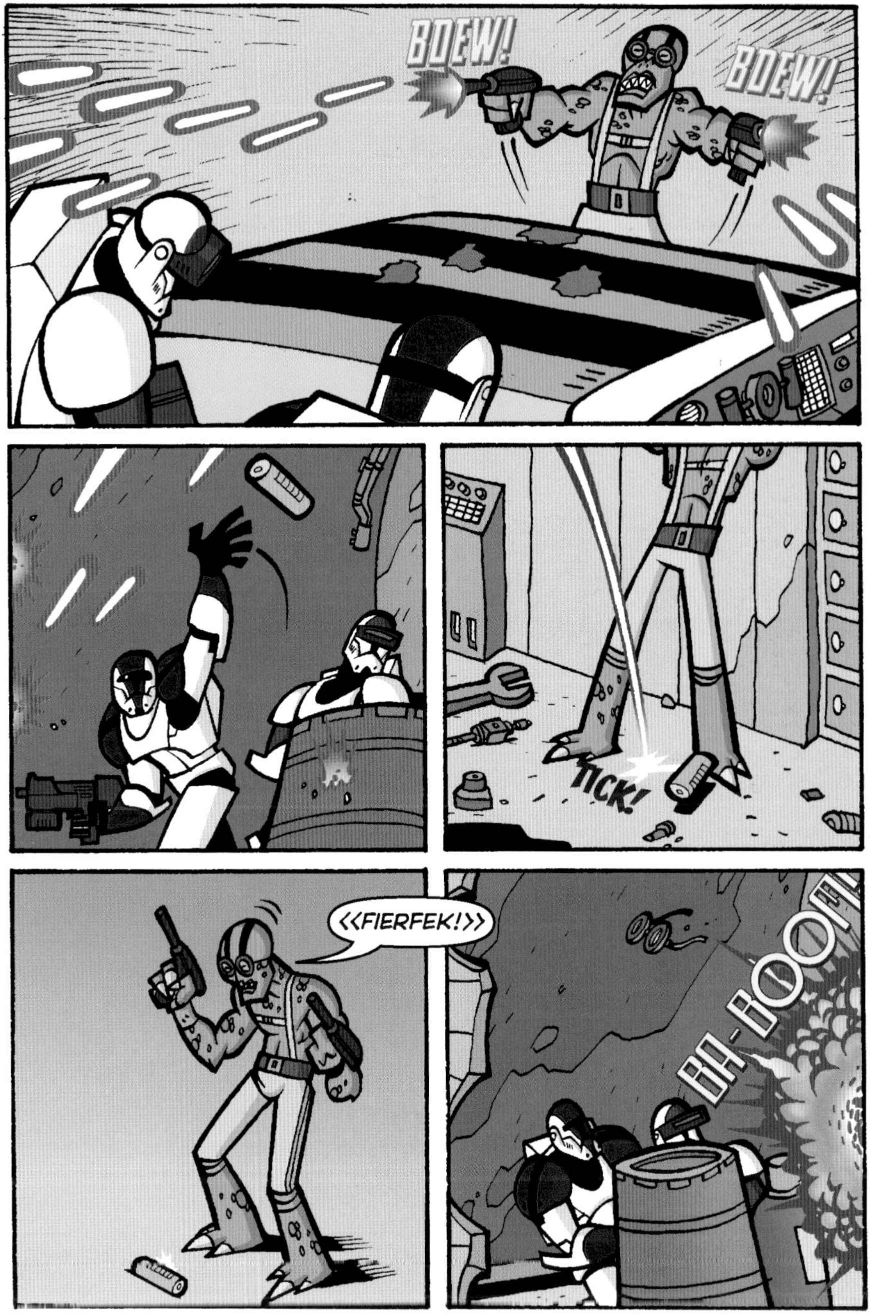
BDEW!
BDEW!
TICK!
<<FIERFEK!>>
BA-BOOM!

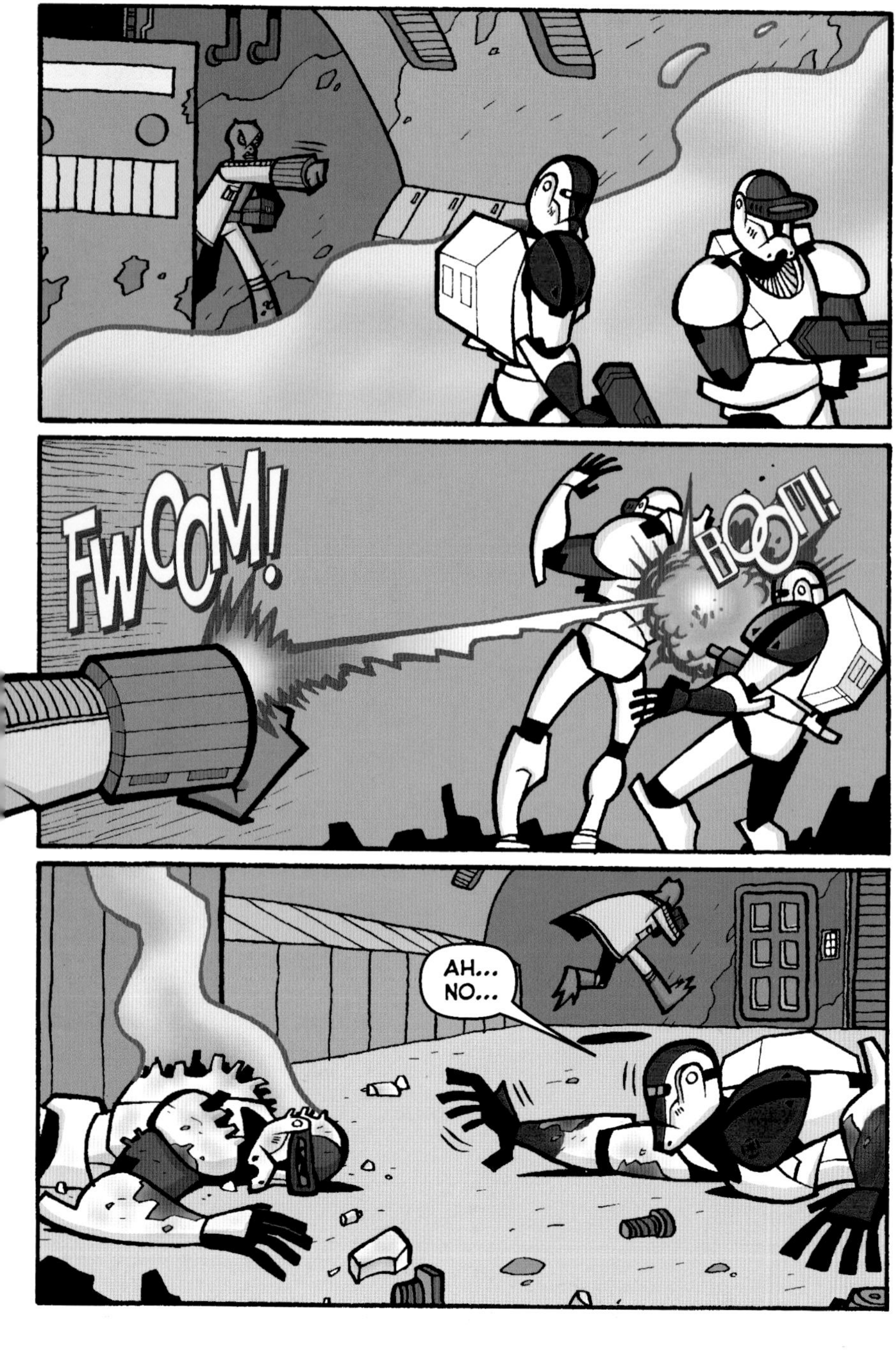
FWOOM!
BOOM!
AH... NO...

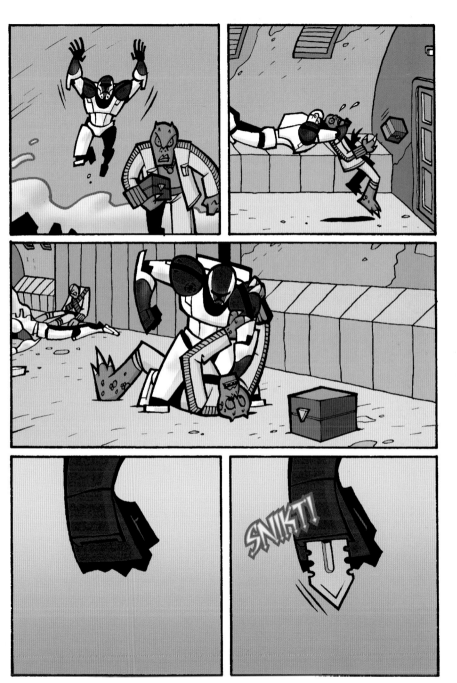

SNIKT!

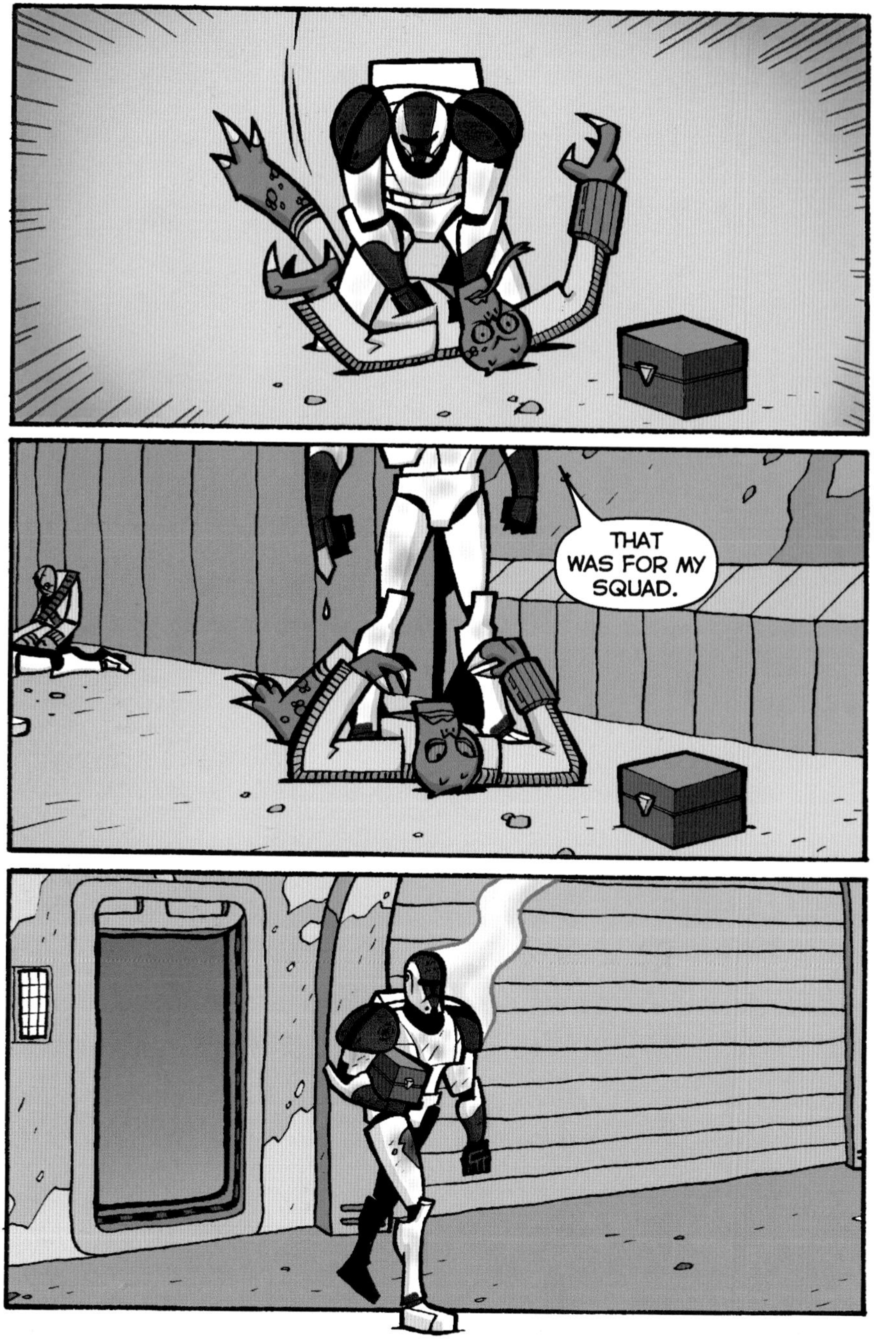
THAT WAS FOR MY SQUAD.

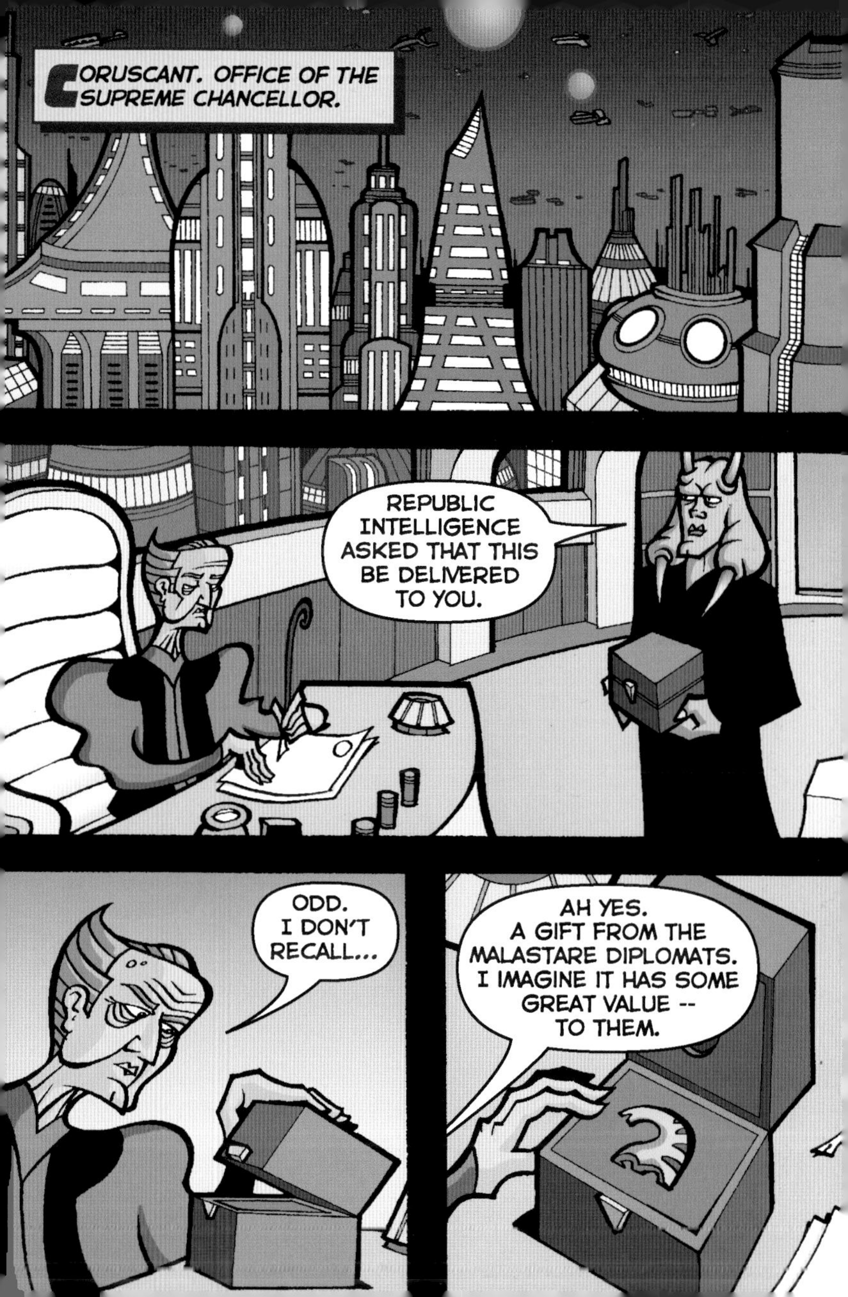
CORUSCANT. OFFICE OF THE SUPREME CHANCELLOR.
REPUBLIC INTELLIGENCE ASKED THAT THIS BE DELIVERED TO YOU.
ODD. I DON'T RECALL...
AH YES. A GIFT FROM THE MALASTARE DIPLOMATS. I IMAGINE IT HAS SOME GREAT VALUE -- TO THEM.

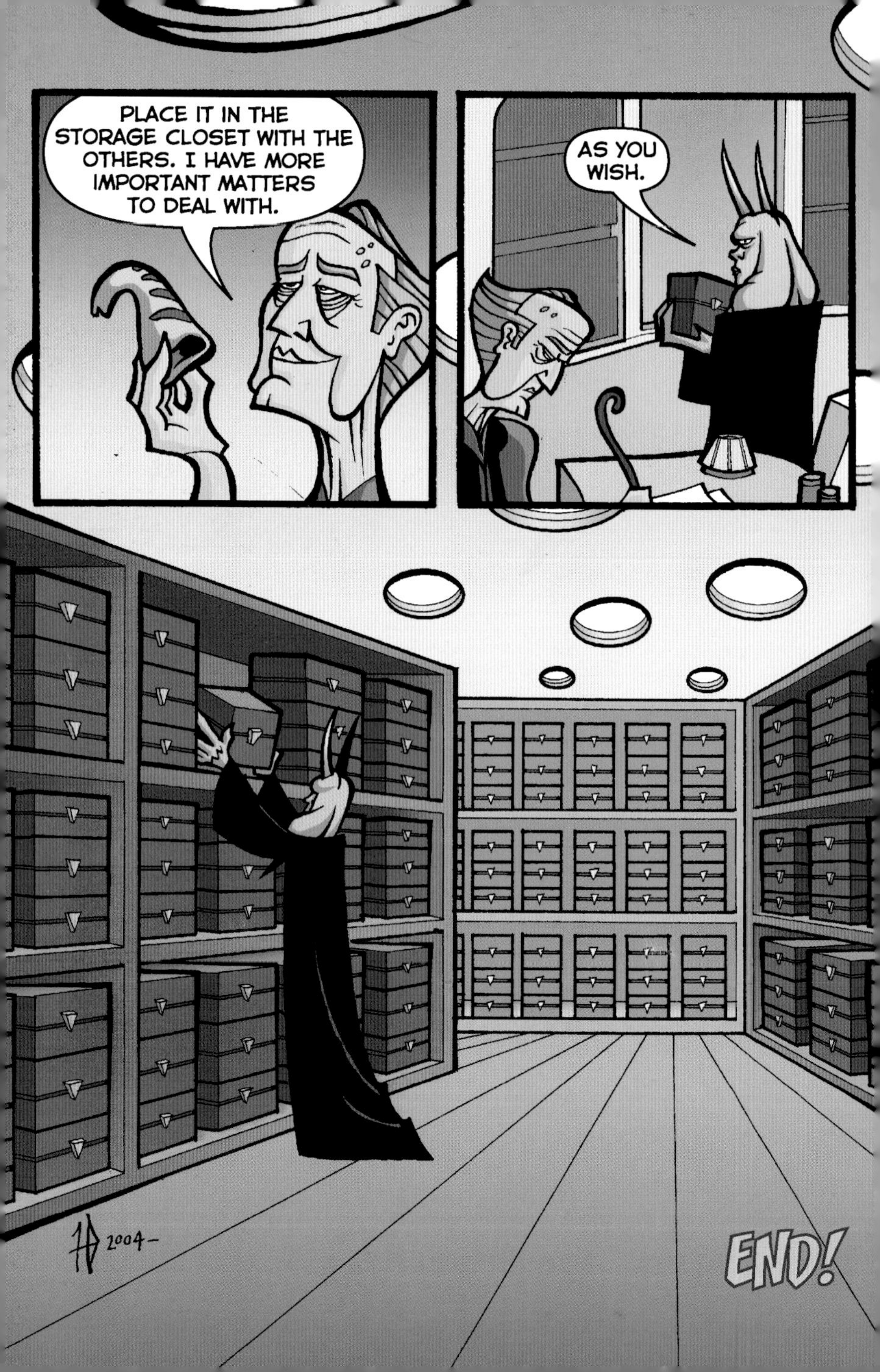
PLACE IT IN THE STORAGE CLOSET WITH THE OTHERS. I HAVE MORE IMPORTANT MATTERS TO DEAL WITH.
AS YOU WISH.
2004
END!

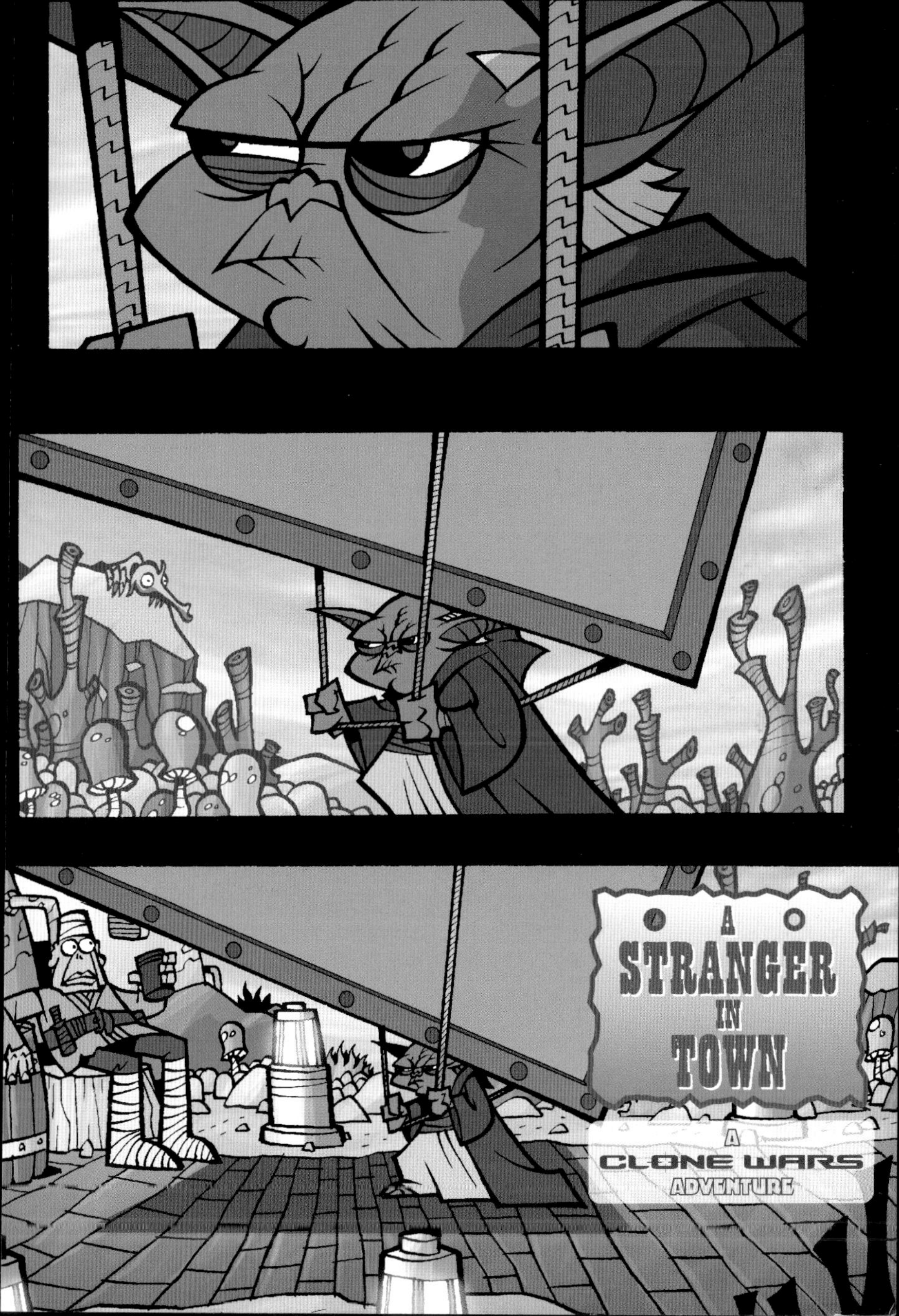
A
STRANGER
IN
TOWN
A
CLONE WARS
ADVENTURE

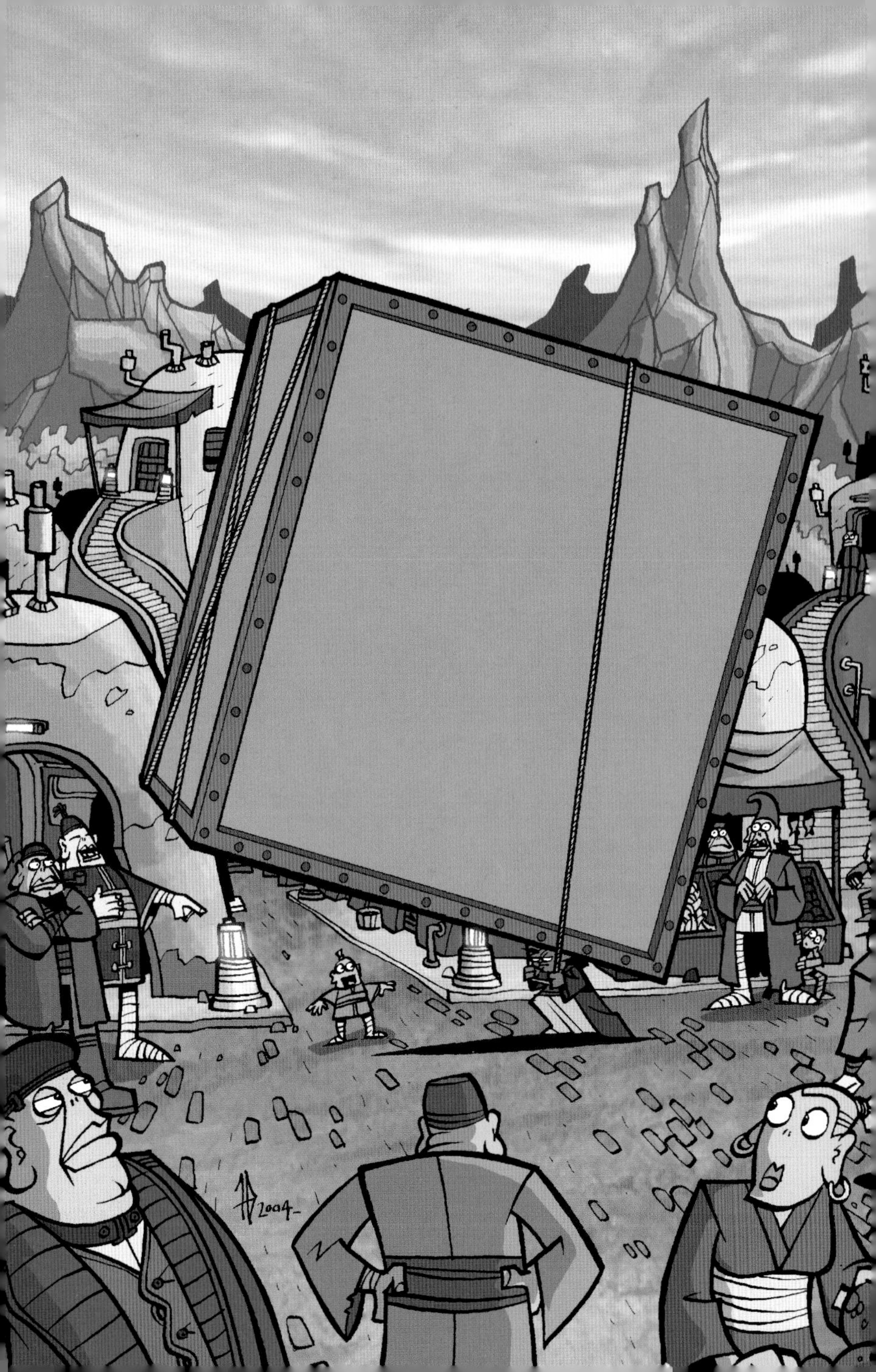

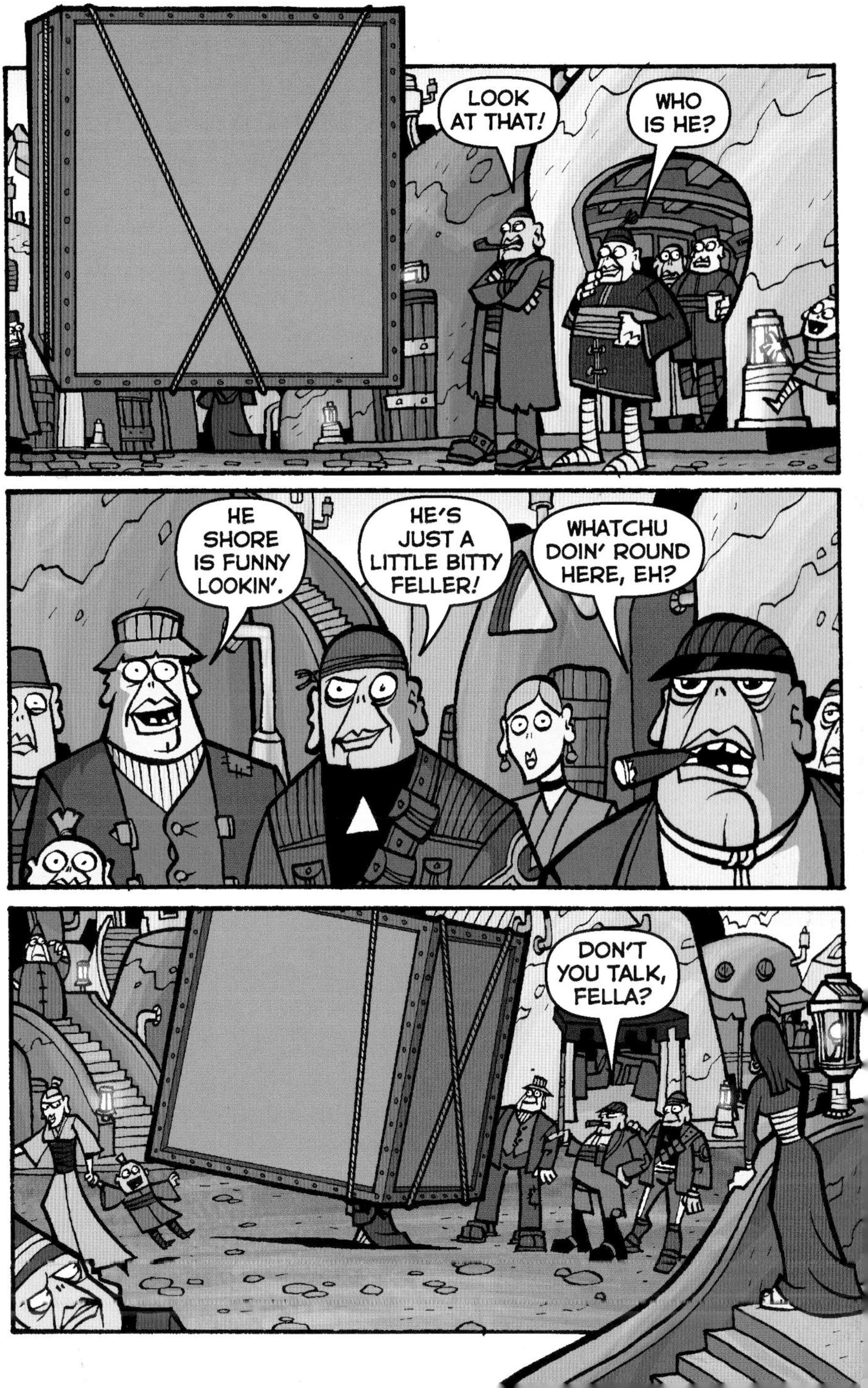
LOOK AT THAT!
WHO IS HE?
HE SHORE IS FUNNY LOOKIN'.
HE'S JUST A LITTLE BITTY FELLER!
WHATCHU DOIN' ROUND HERE, EH?
DON'T YOU TALK, FELLA?

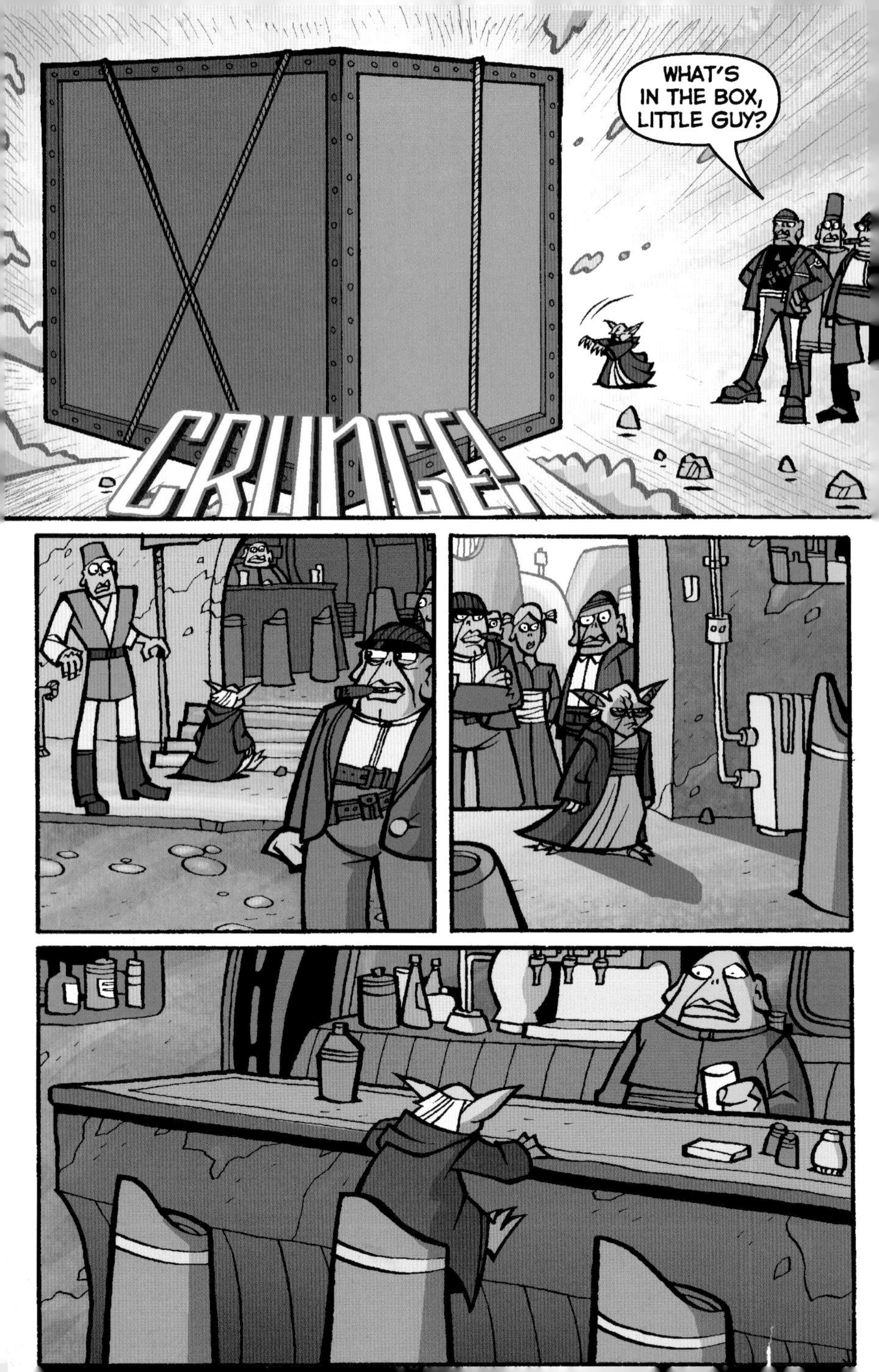
WHAT'S IN THE BOX, LITTLE GUY?
CRUNCH!

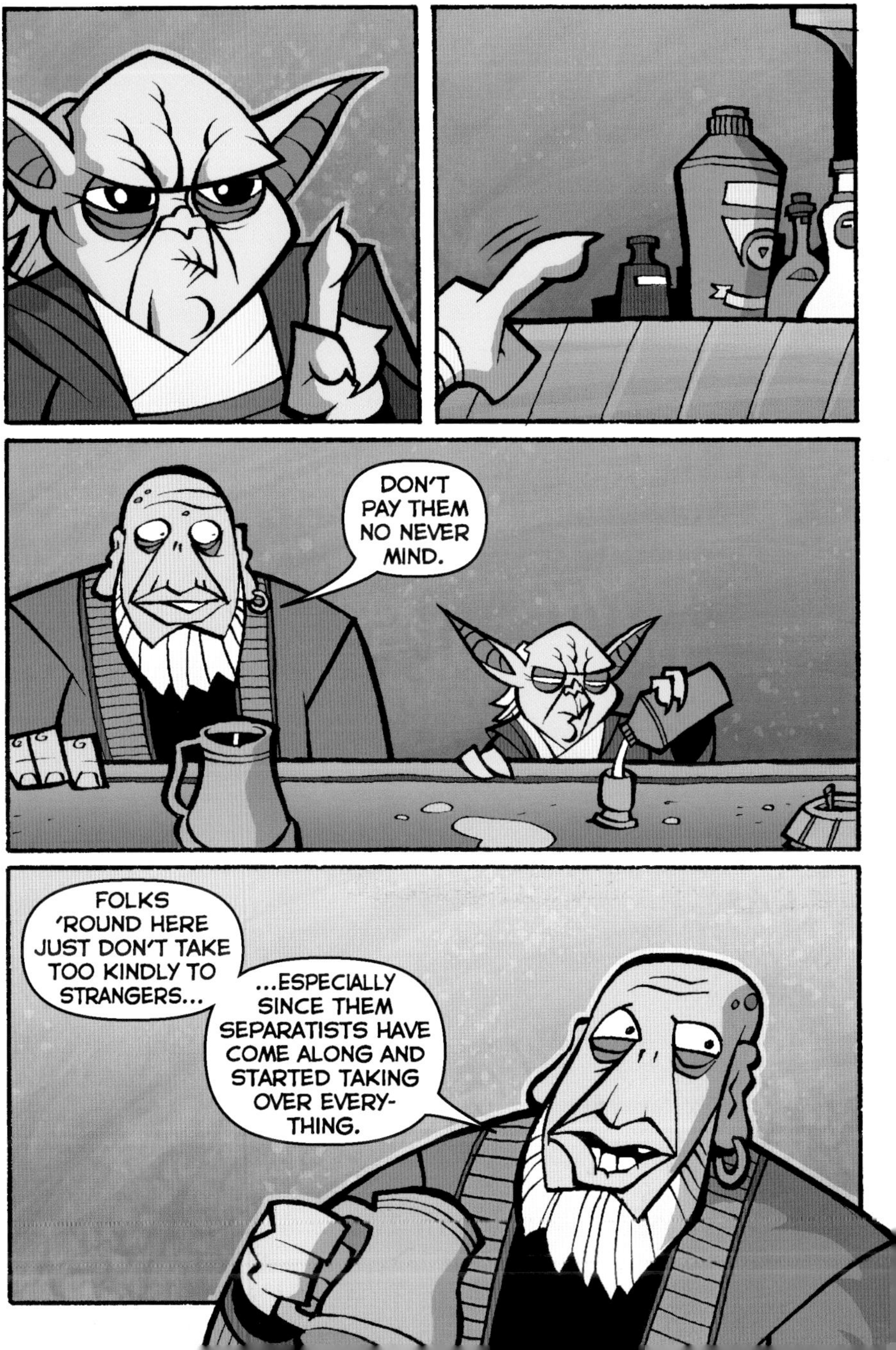
DON'T PAY THEM NO NEVER MIND.
FOLKS 'ROUND HERE JUST DON'T TAKE TOO KINDLY TO STRANGERS...
...ESPECIALLY SINCE THEM SEPARATISTS HAVE COME ALONG AND STARTED TAKING OVER EVERY-THING.

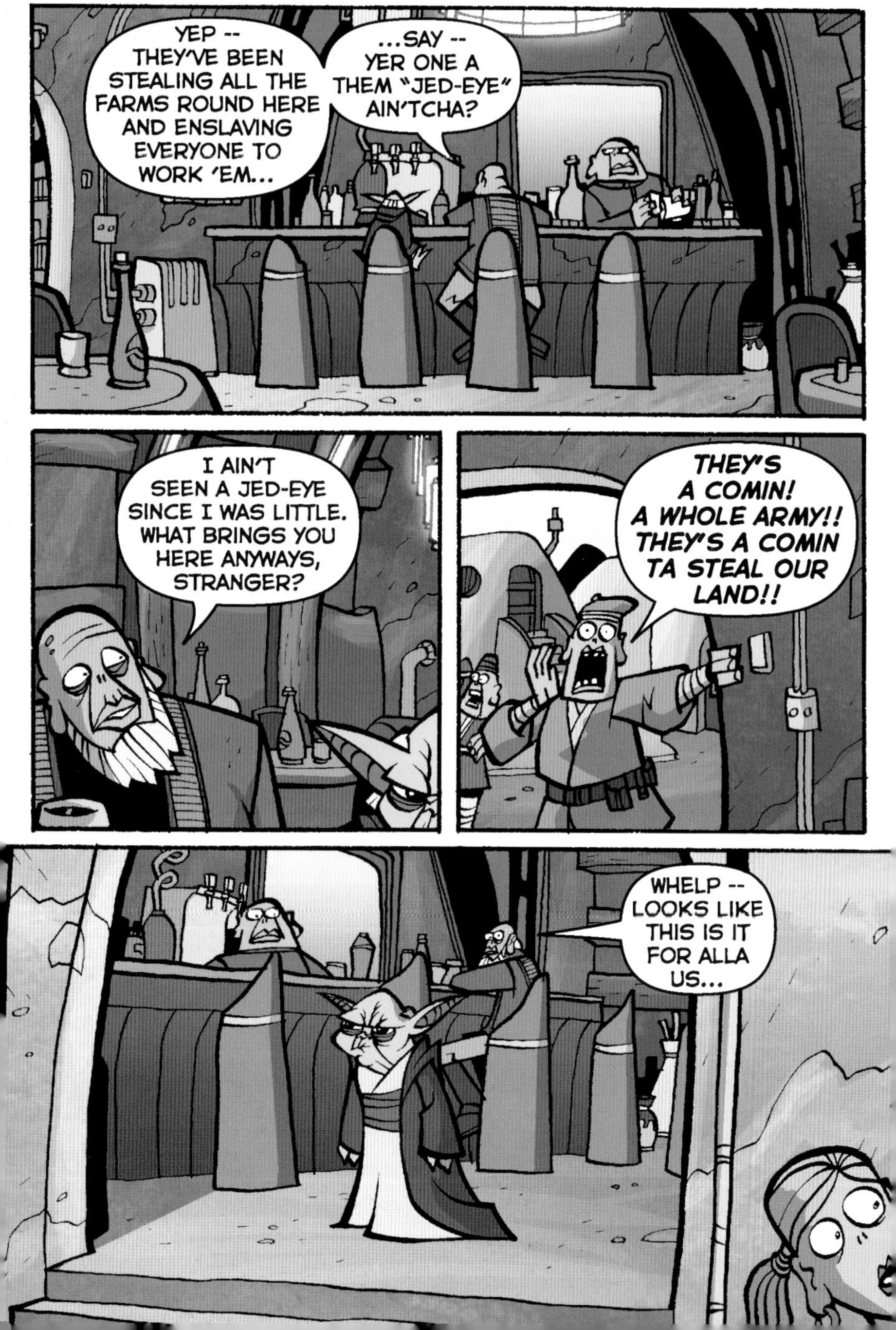
YEP -- THEY'VE BEEN STEALING ALL THE FARMS ROUND HERE AND ENSLAVING EVERYONE TO WORK 'EM...
...SAY -- YER ONE A THEM "JED-EYE" AIN'TCHA?
I AIN'T SEEN A JED-EYE SINCE I WAS LITTLE. WHAT BRINGS YOU HERE ANYWAYS, STRANGER?
THEY'S A COMIN! A WHOLE ARMY!! THEY'S A COMIN TA STEAL OUR LAND!!
WHELP -- LOOKS LIKE THIS IS IT FOR ALLA US...

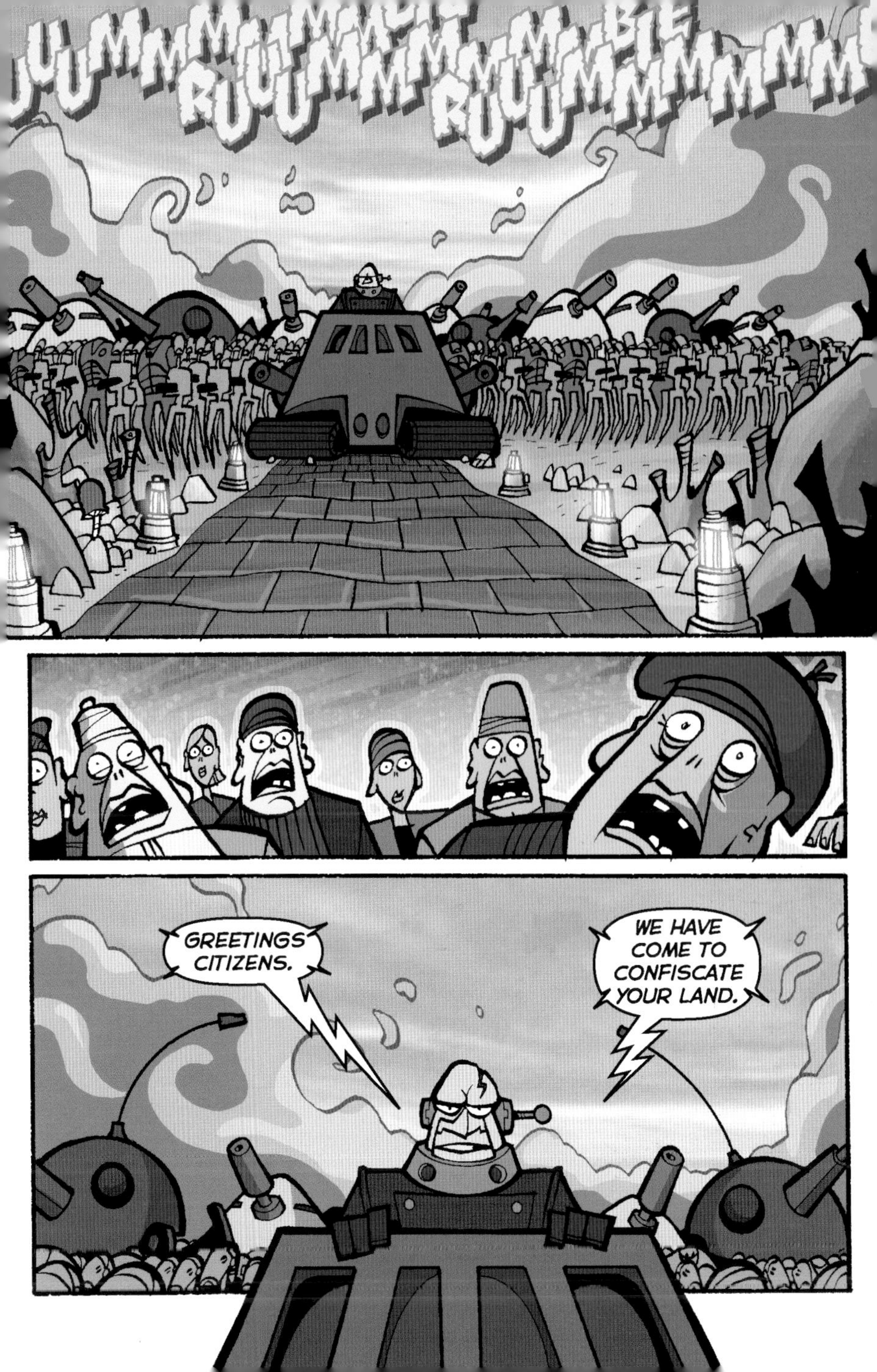
GREETINGS CITIZENS.
WE HAVE COME TO CONFISCATE YOUR LAND.

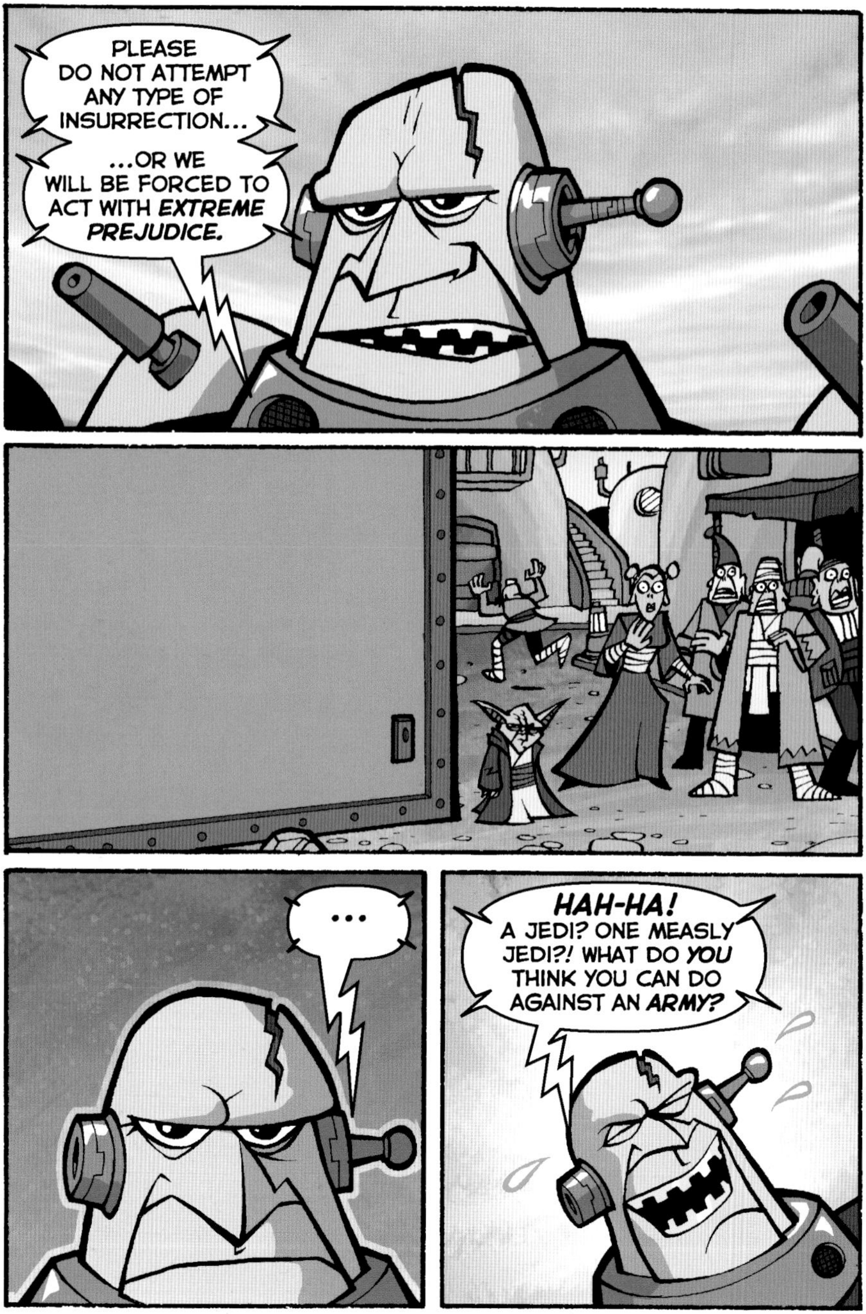
PLEASE DO NOT ATTEMPT ANY TYPE OF INSURRECTION...
...OR WE WILL BE FORCED TO ACT WITH *EXTREME PREJUDICE.*
...
HAH-HA! A JEDI? ONE MEASLY JEDI?! WHAT DO *YOU* THINK YOU CAN DO AGAINST AN *ARMY?*

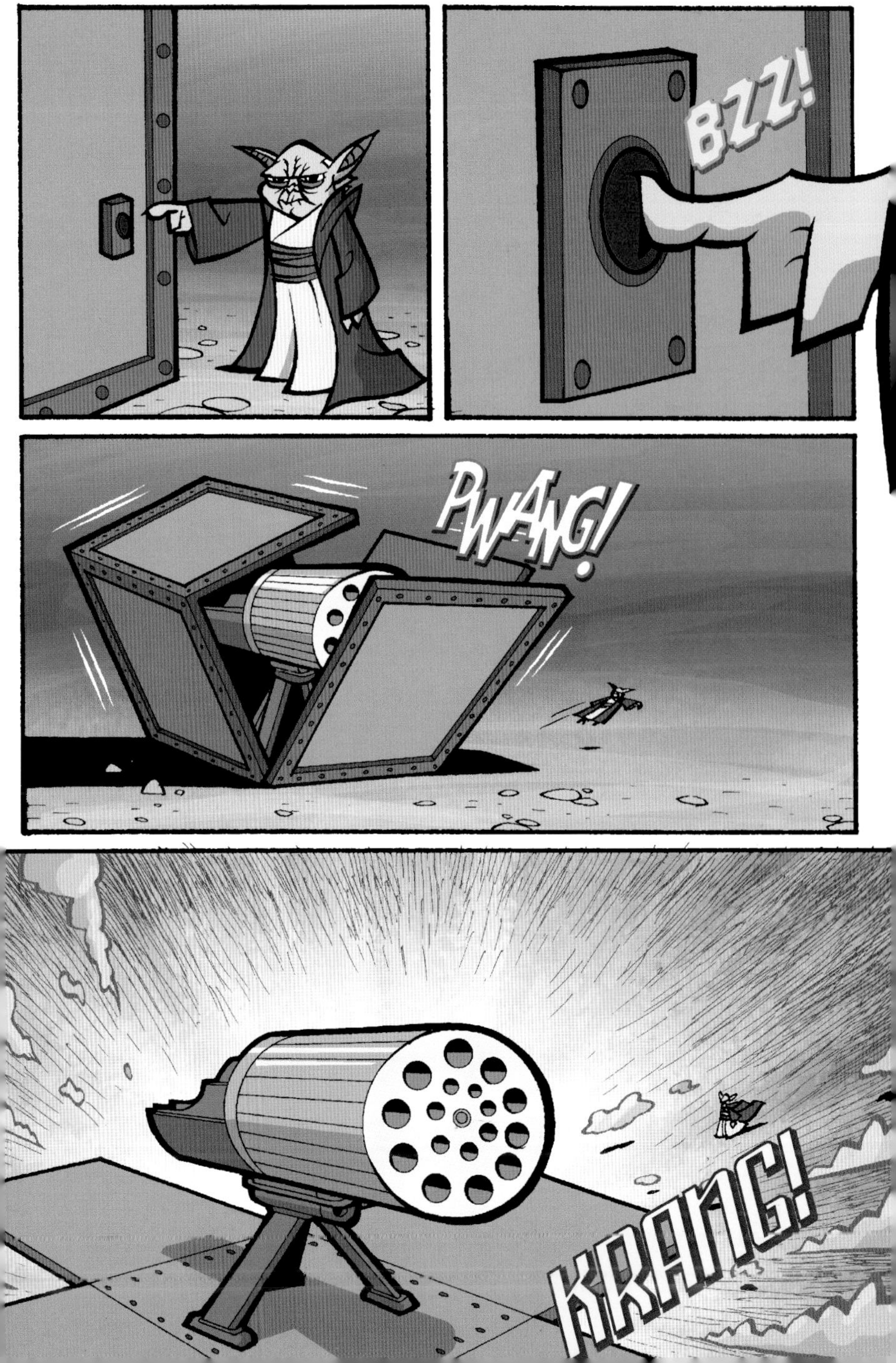
BZZ!
PWANG!
KRANG!

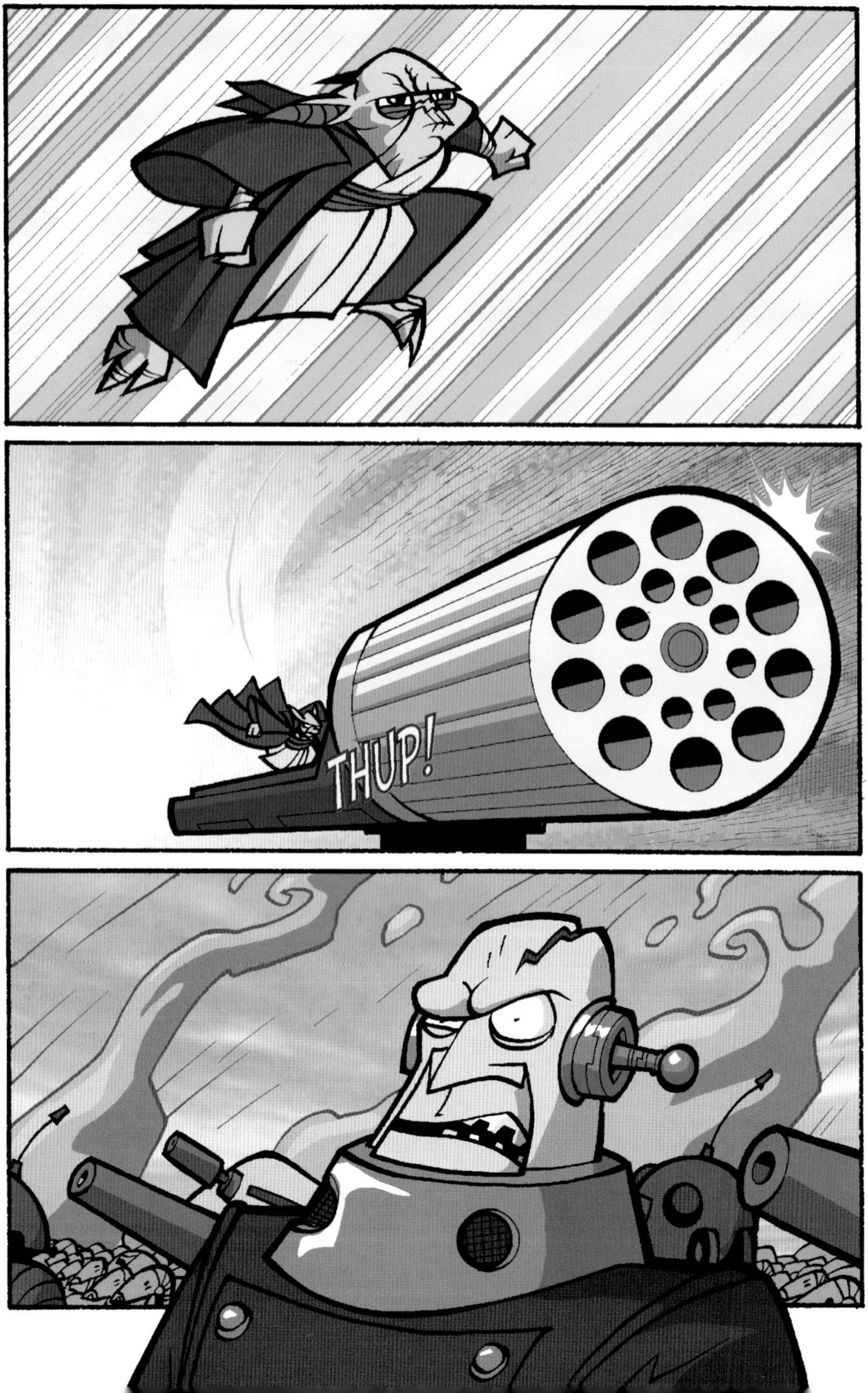
THUP!

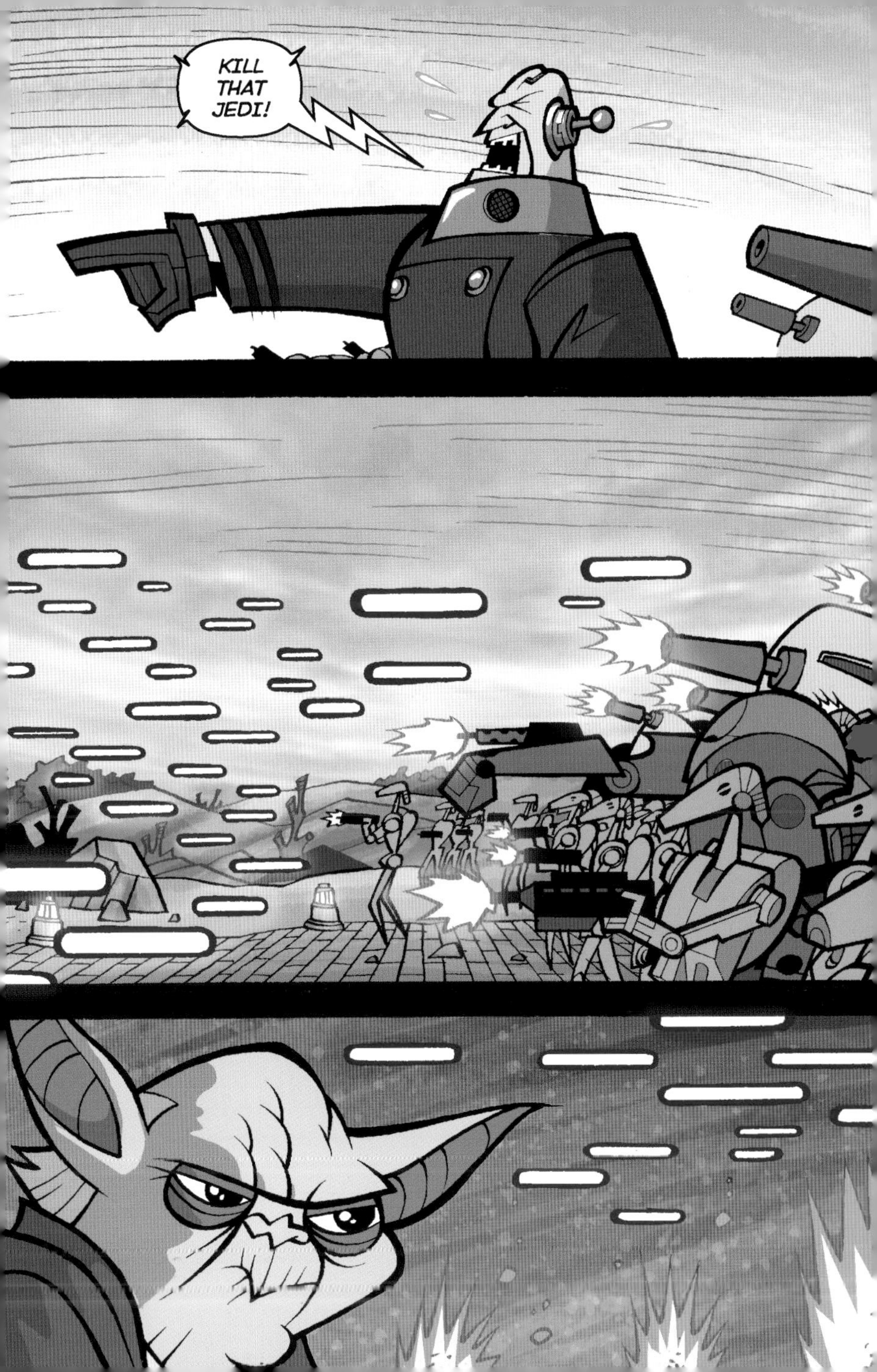
KILL THAT JEDI!

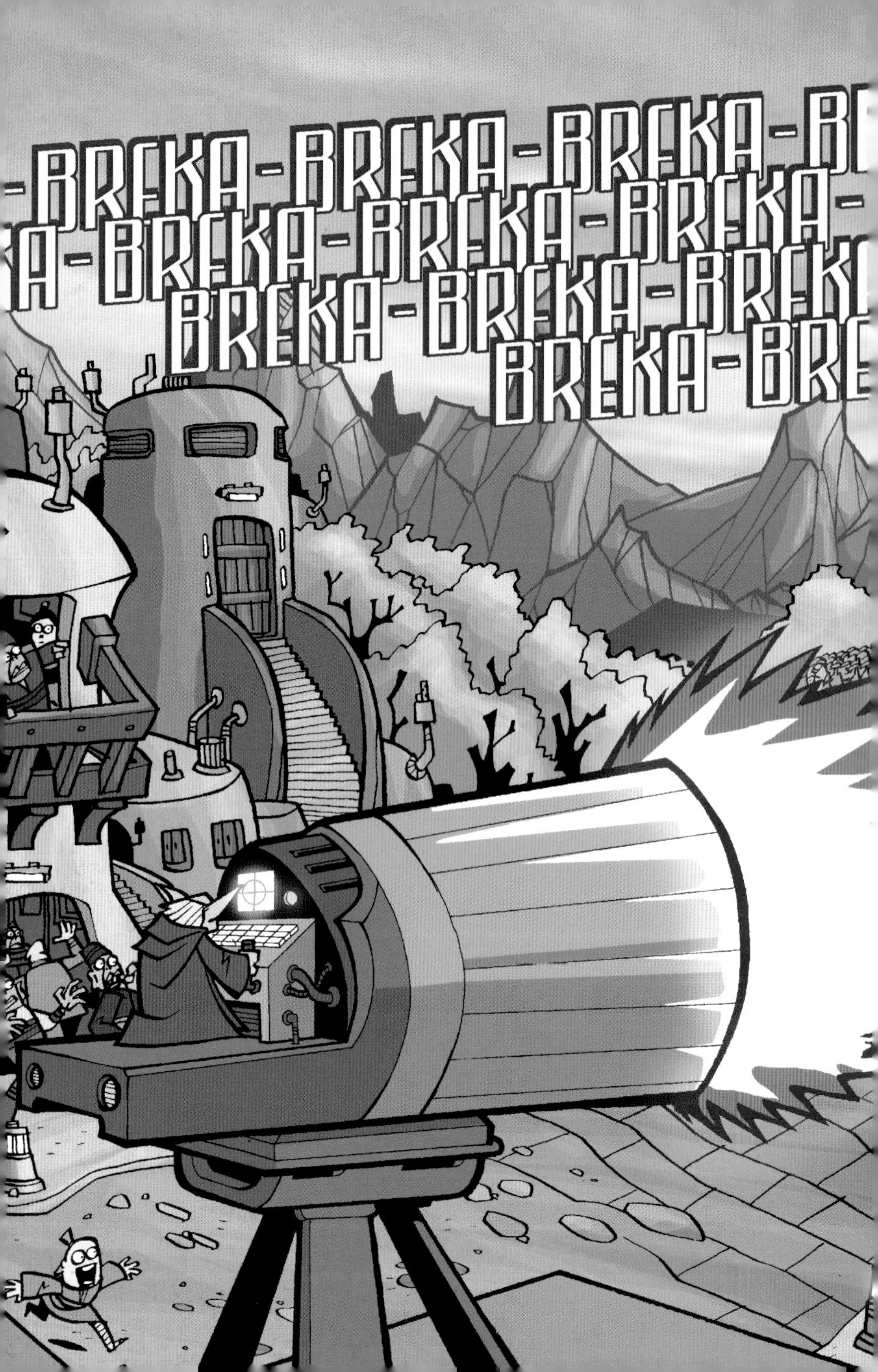
-BREKA-BREKA-BREKA-
-BREKA-BREKA-BREKA-
BREKA-BREKA-
BREKA-

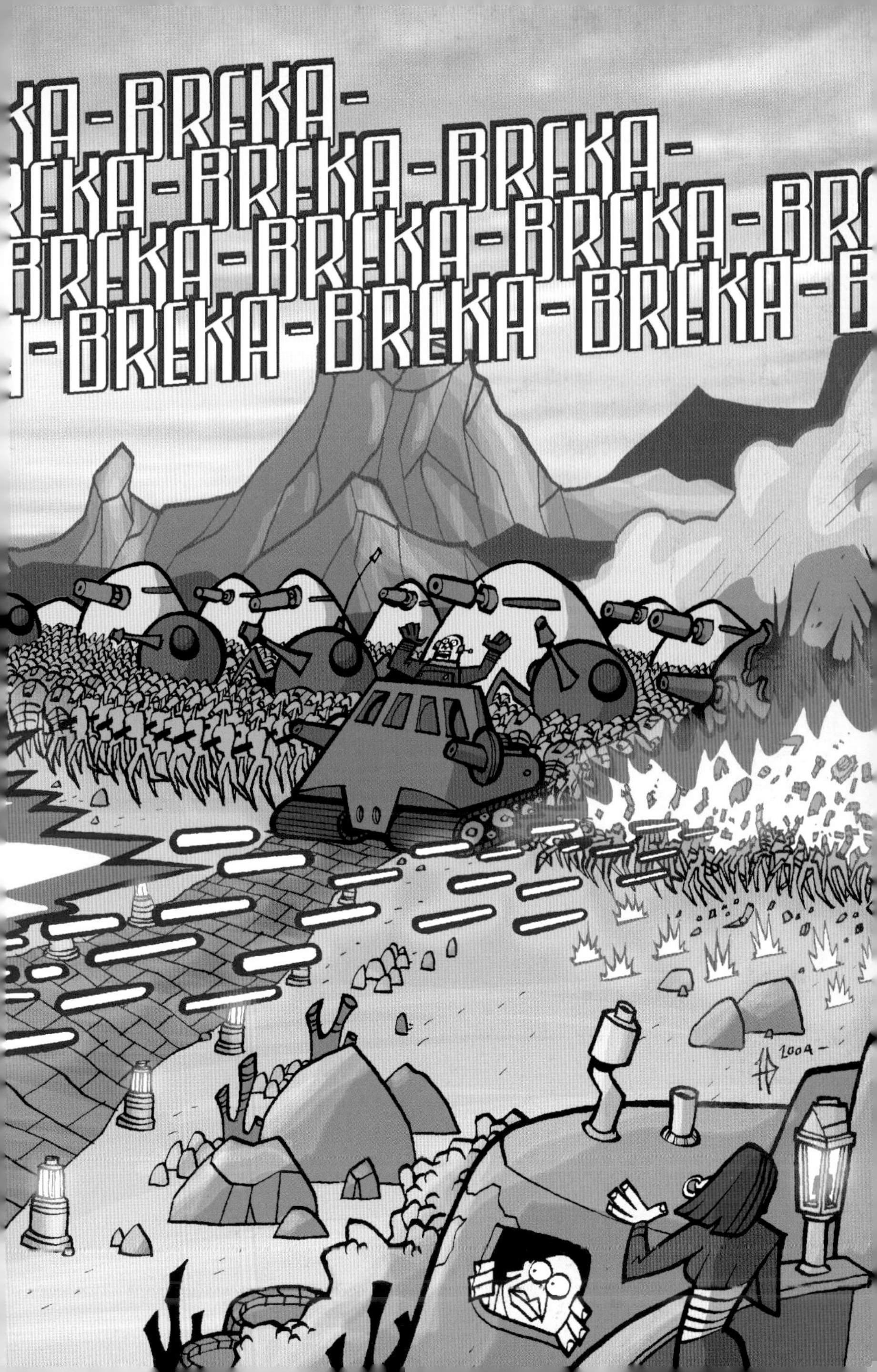

KA-BREKA-
REKA-BREKA-BREKA-
BREKA-BREKA-BREKA-BR
-BREKA-BREKA-BREKA-B
2004

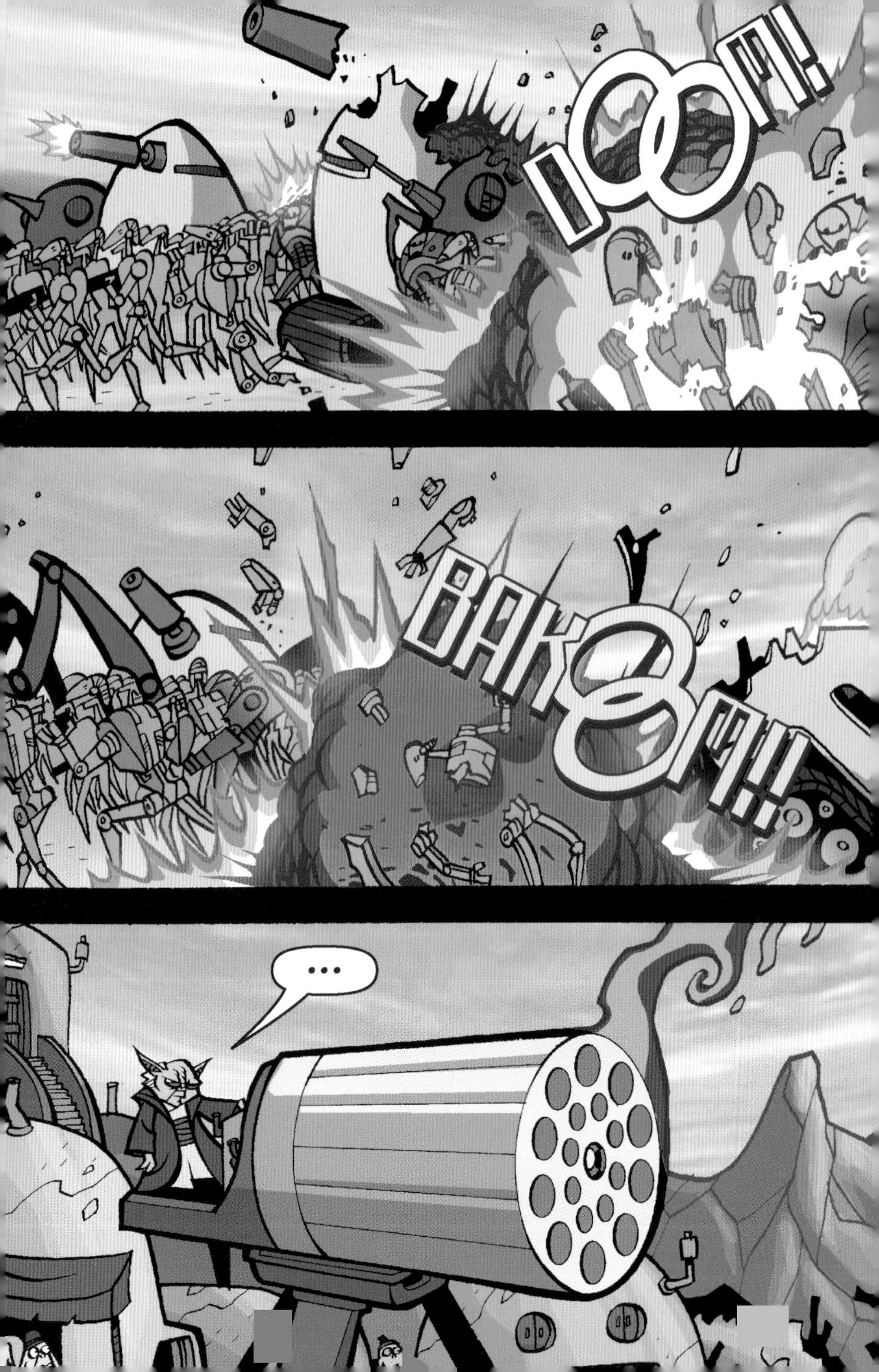
DOOM!!
BAKOOM!!
...

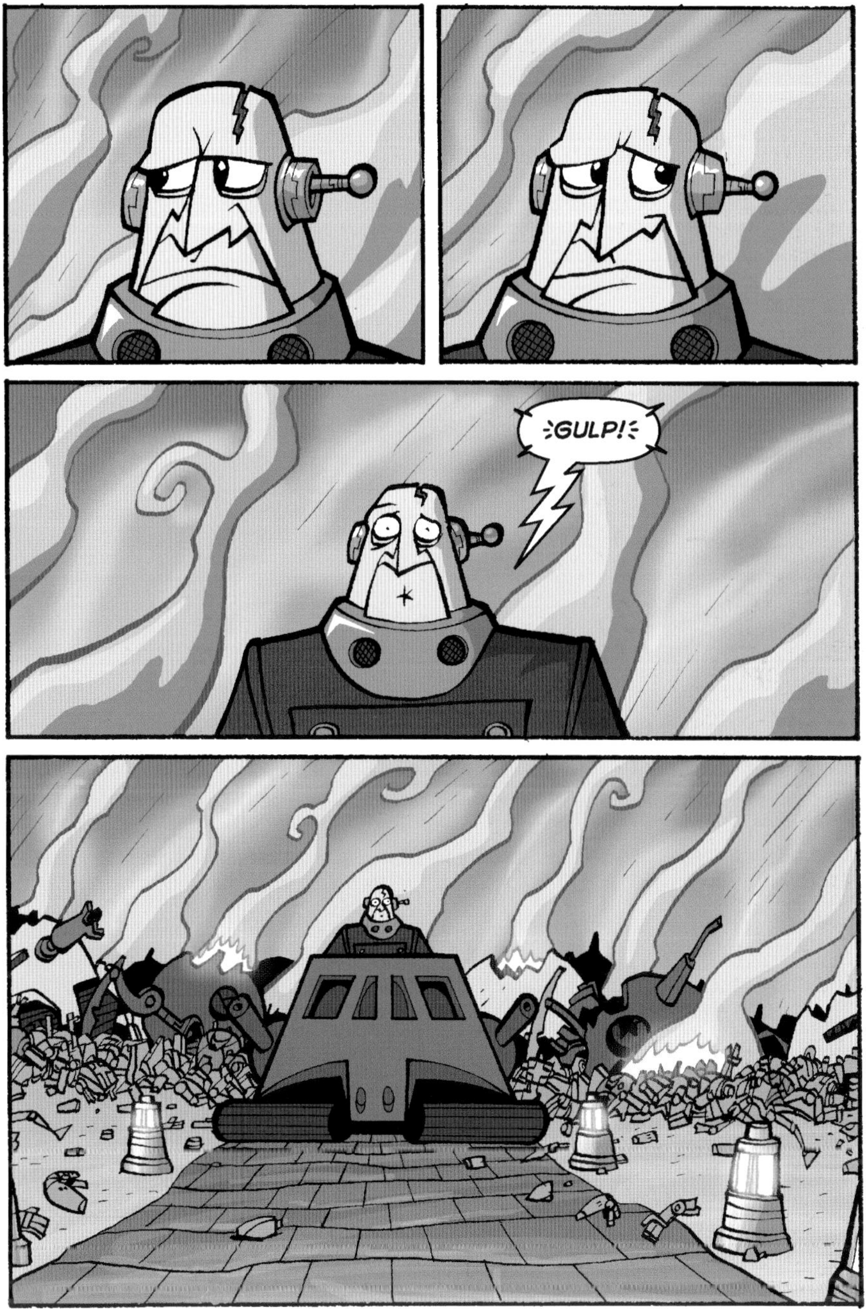
GULP!

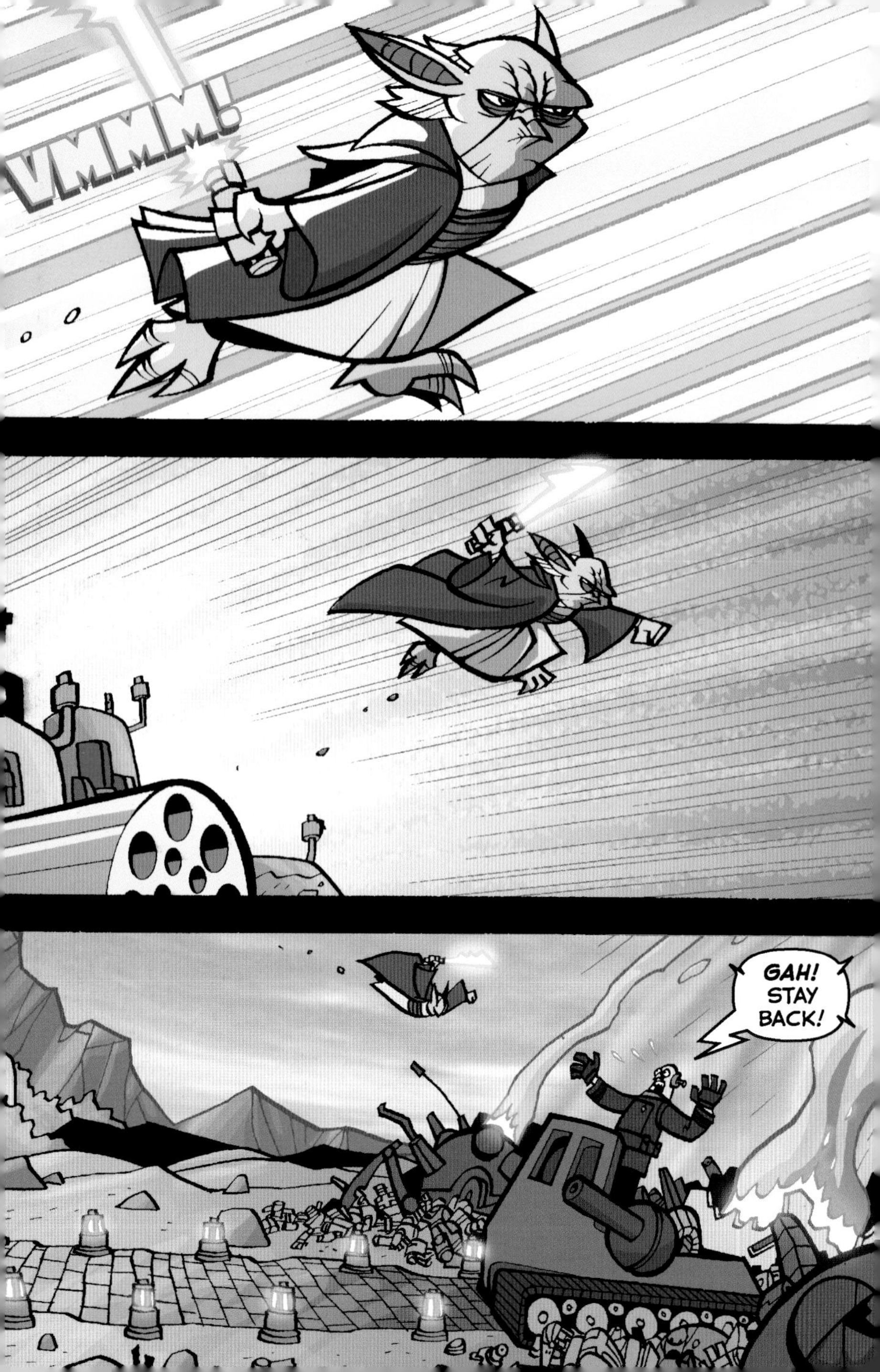
VMMM!
GAH! STAY BACK!

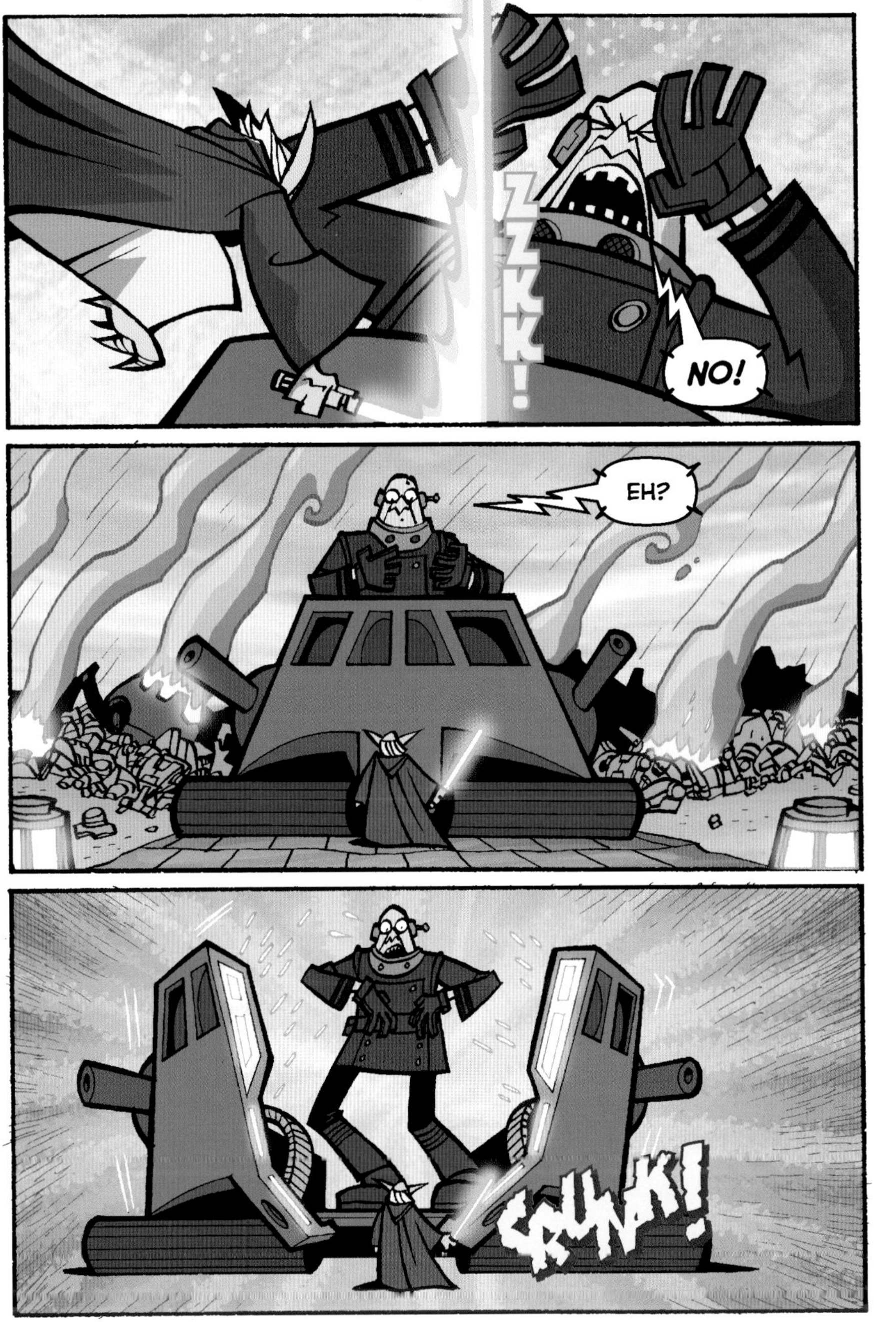
ZZKK!
NO!
EH?
CRUNK!

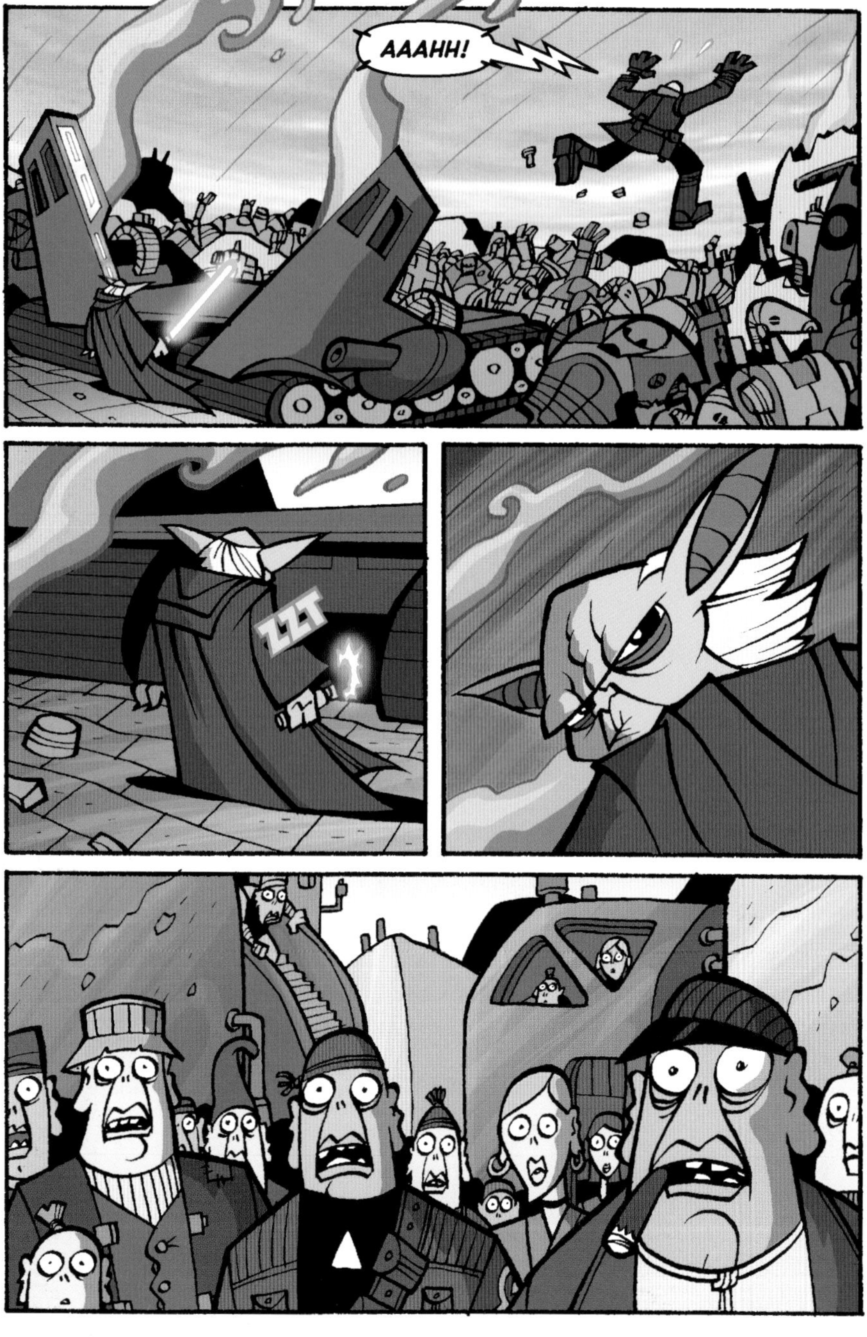
AAAHH!
ZZT

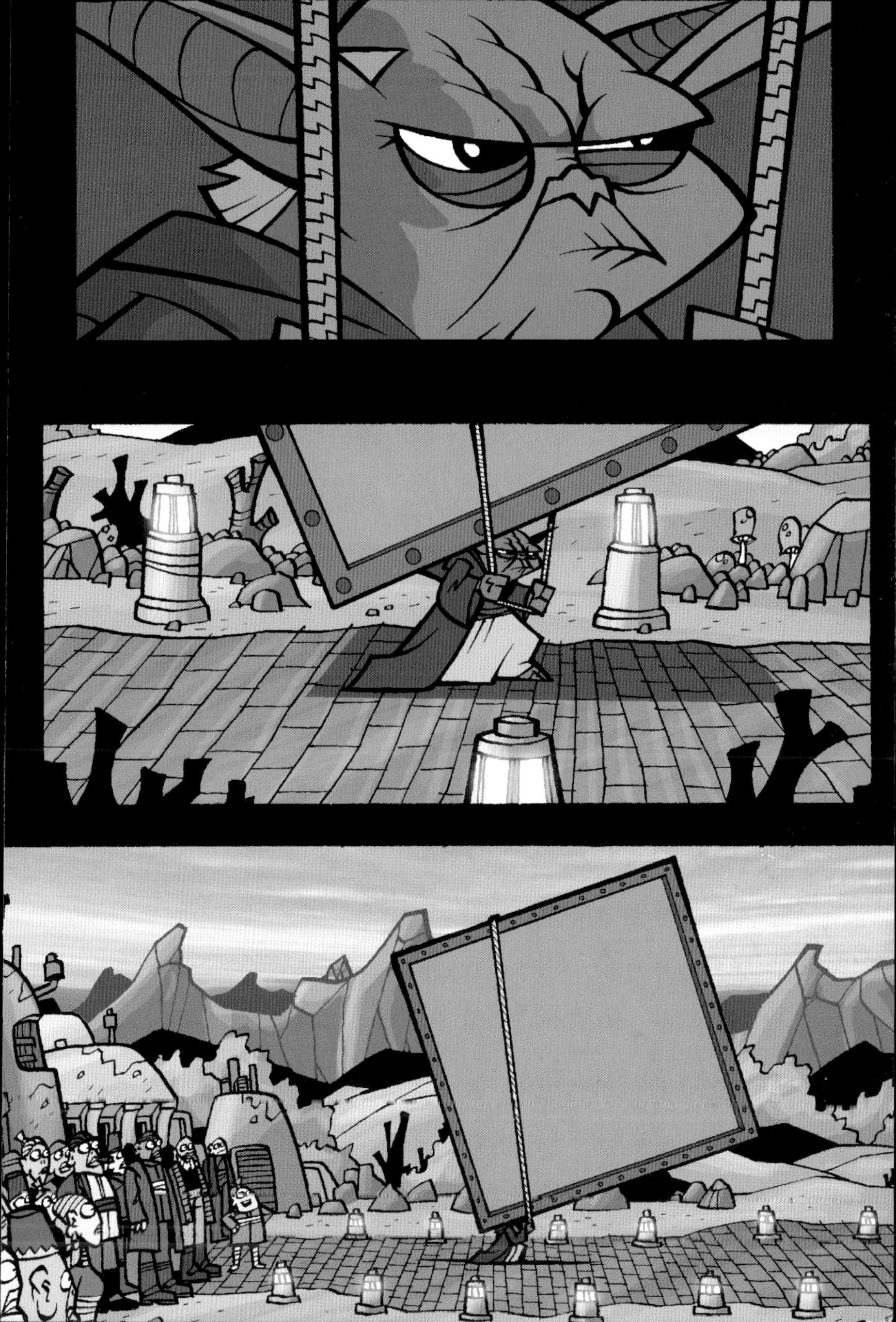

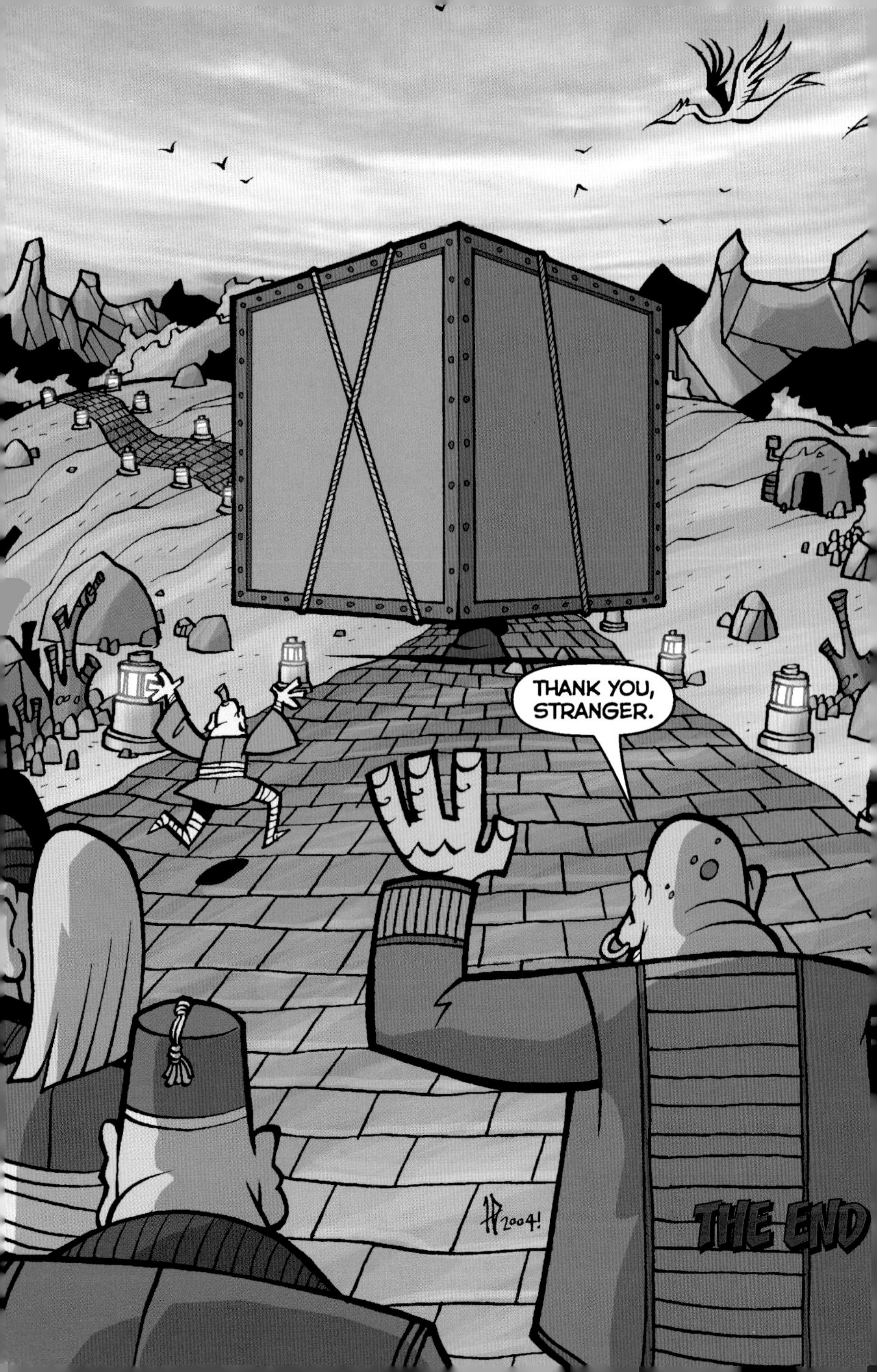
THANK YOU, STRANGER.
THE END

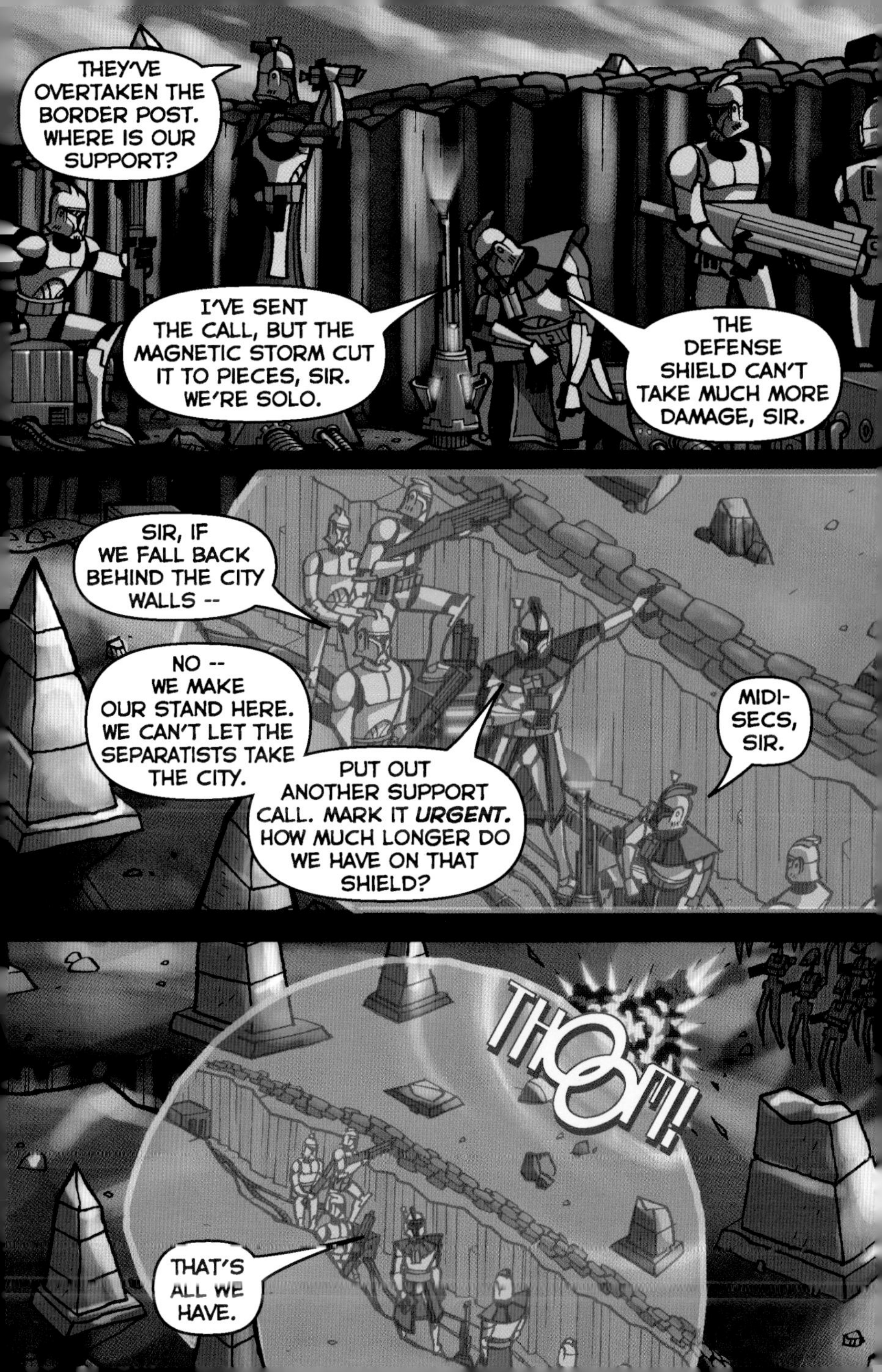
THEY'VE OVERTAKEN THE BORDER POST. WHERE IS OUR SUPPORT?
I'VE SENT THE CALL, BUT THE MAGNETIC STORM CUT IT TO PIECES, SIR. WE'RE SOLO.
THE DEFENSE SHIELD CAN'T TAKE MUCH MORE DAMAGE, SIR.
SIR, IF WE FALL BACK BEHIND THE CITY WALLS --
NO -- WE MAKE OUR STAND HERE. WE CAN'T LET THE SEPARATISTS TAKE THE CITY.
PUT OUT ANOTHER SUPPORT CALL. MARK IT *URGENT.* HOW MUCH LONGER DO WE HAVE ON THAT SHIELD?
MIDI-SECS, SIR.
THOOM!
THAT'S ALL WE HAVE.

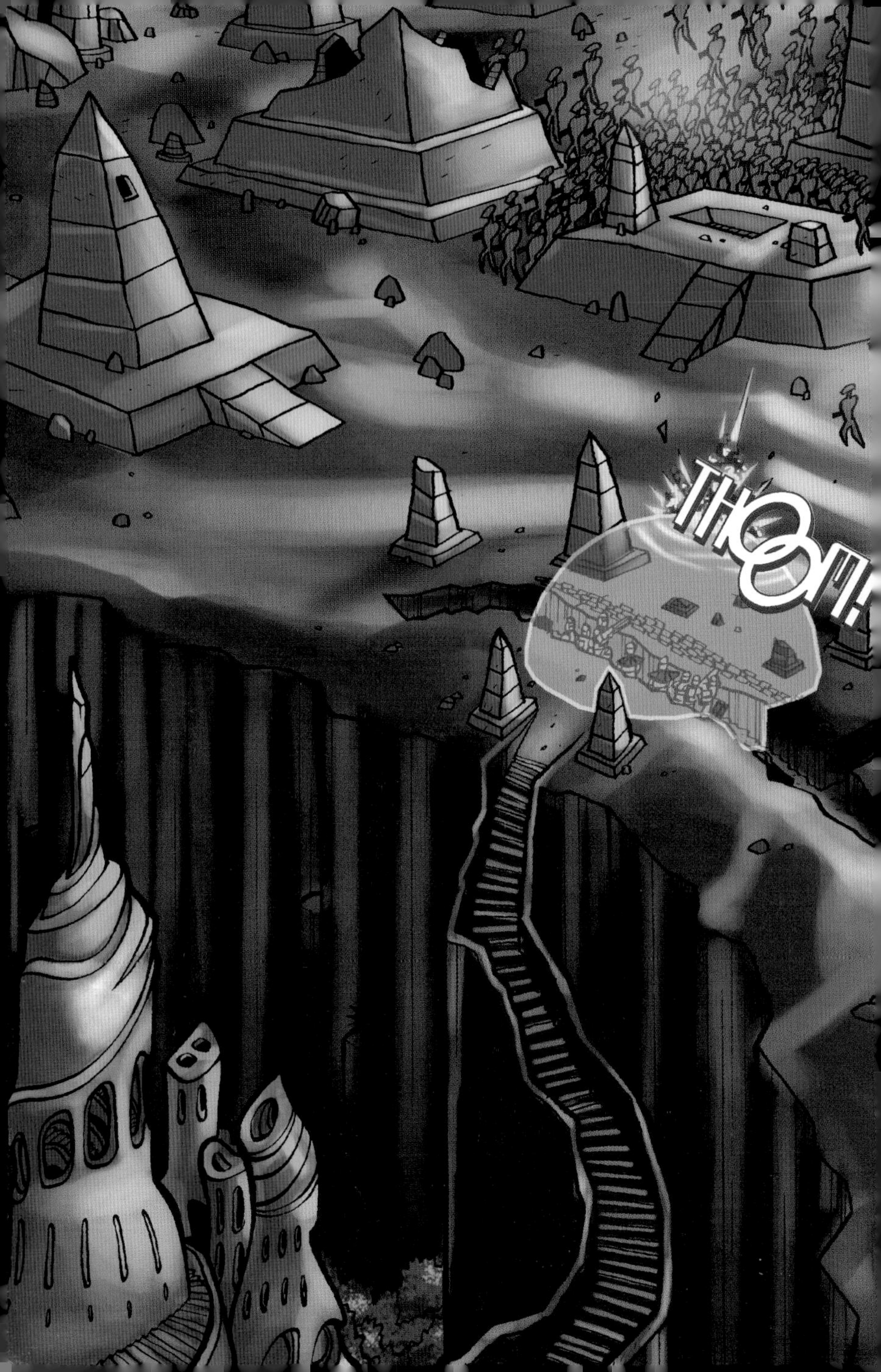
THOOM!

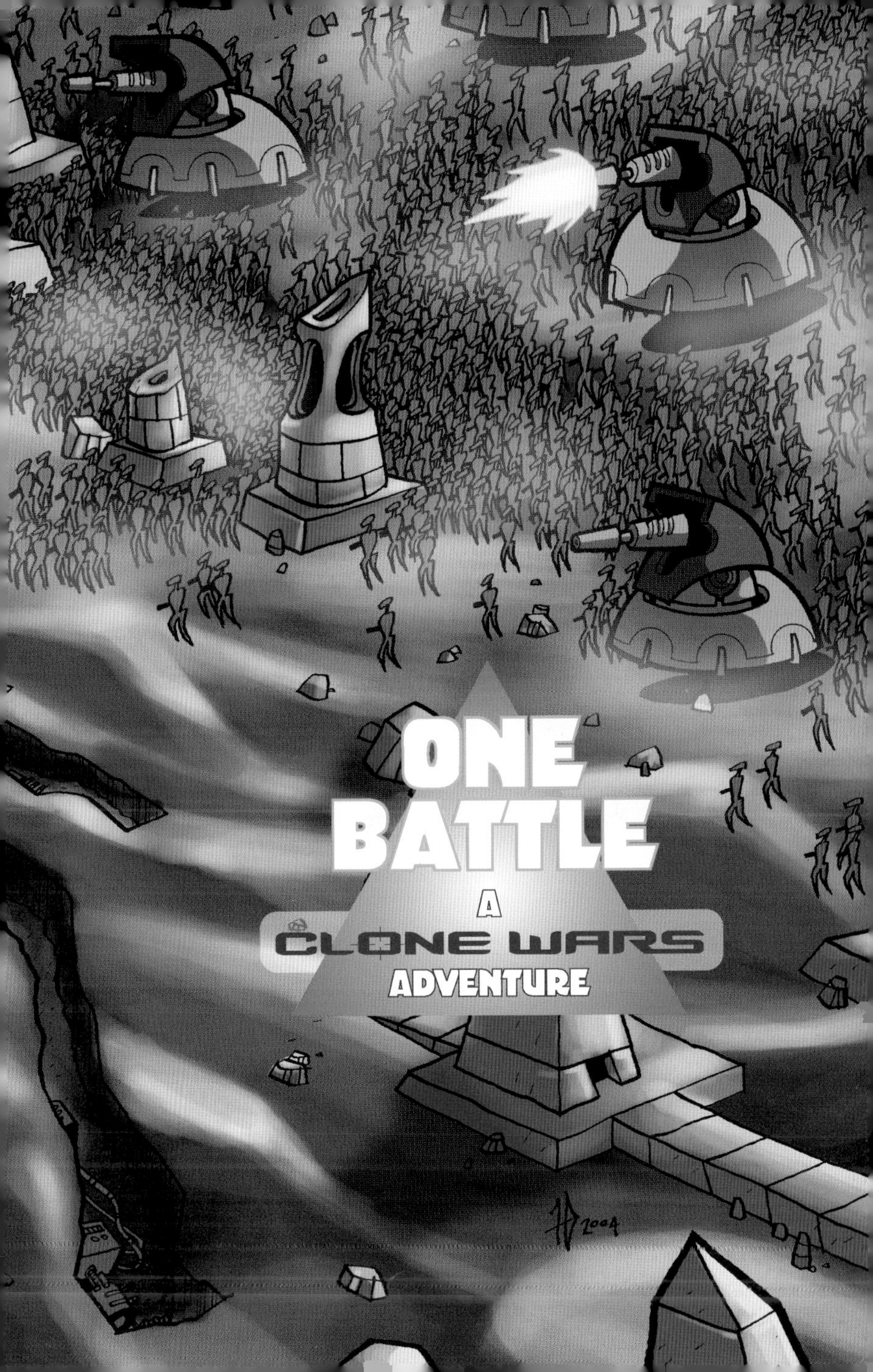
ONE BATTLE
A
CLONE WARS
ADVENTURE

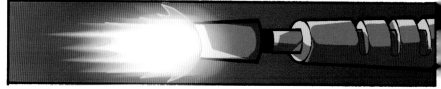

BRACE FOR IMPACT!

KRA-THOOM!

DON'T WAIT FOR THE SMOKE TO CLEAR -- SEND THEM TO THE TRASH COMPACTORS!

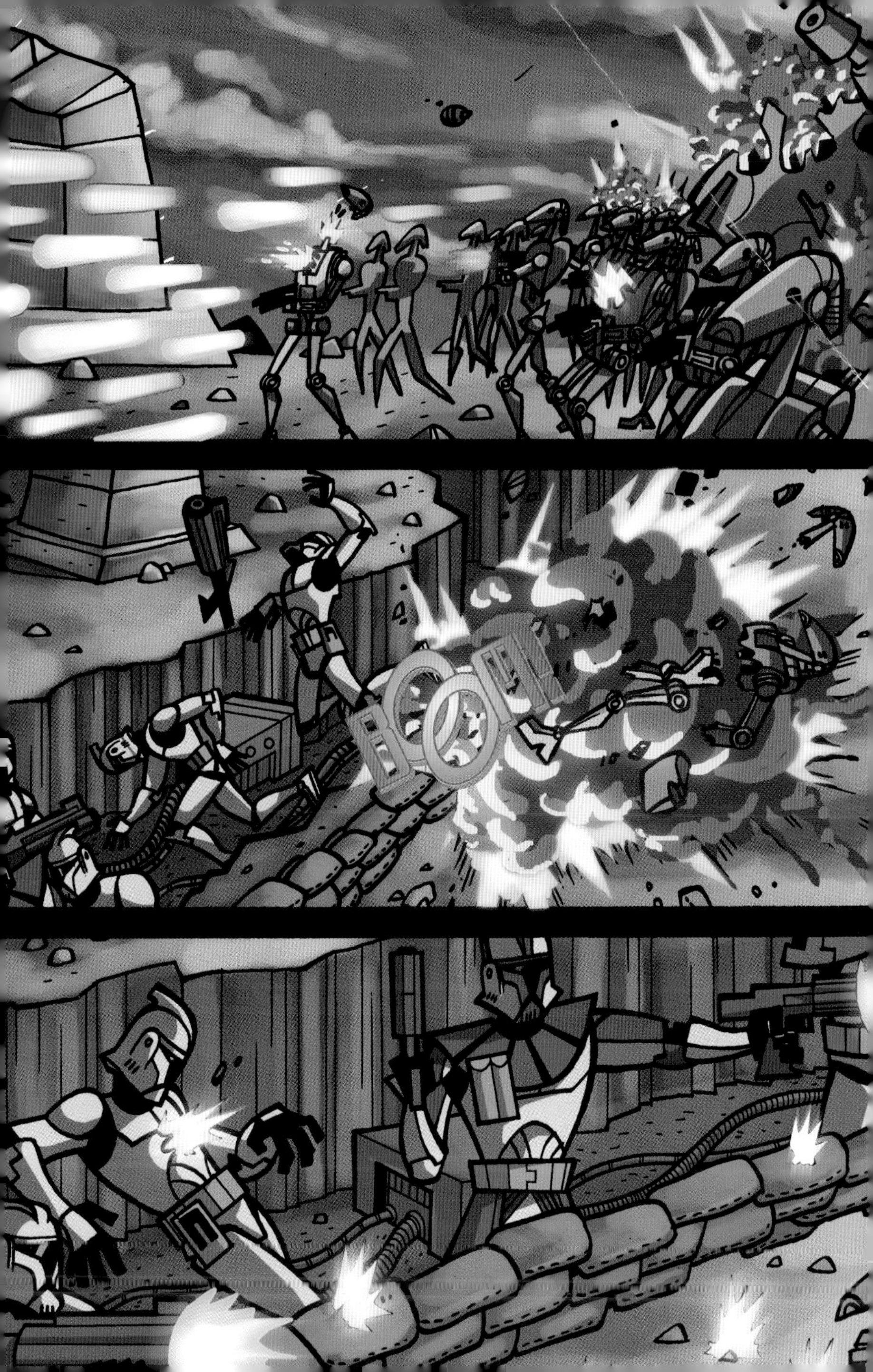
BOOM!

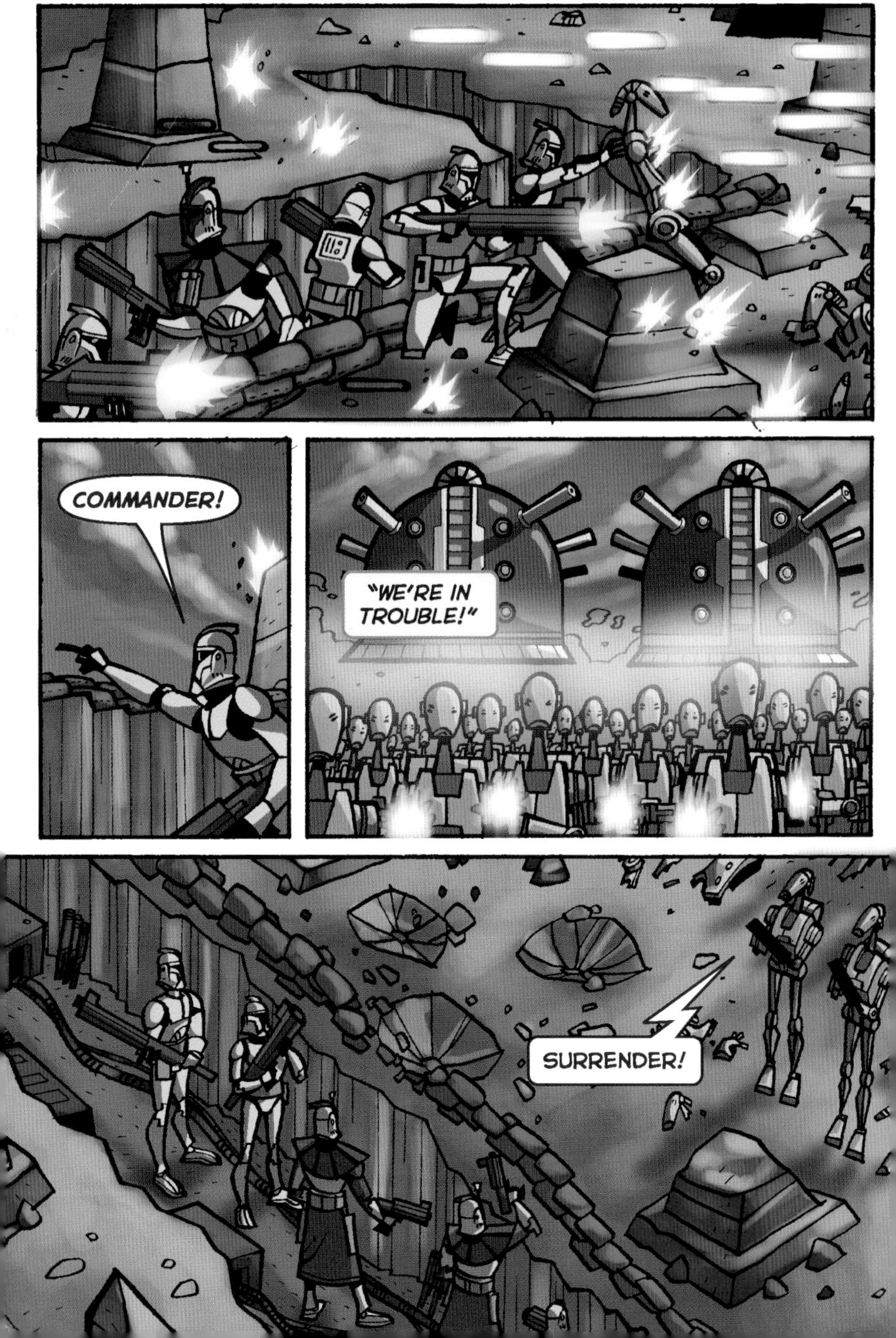
COMMANDER!
"WE'RE IN TROUBLE!"
SURRENDER!

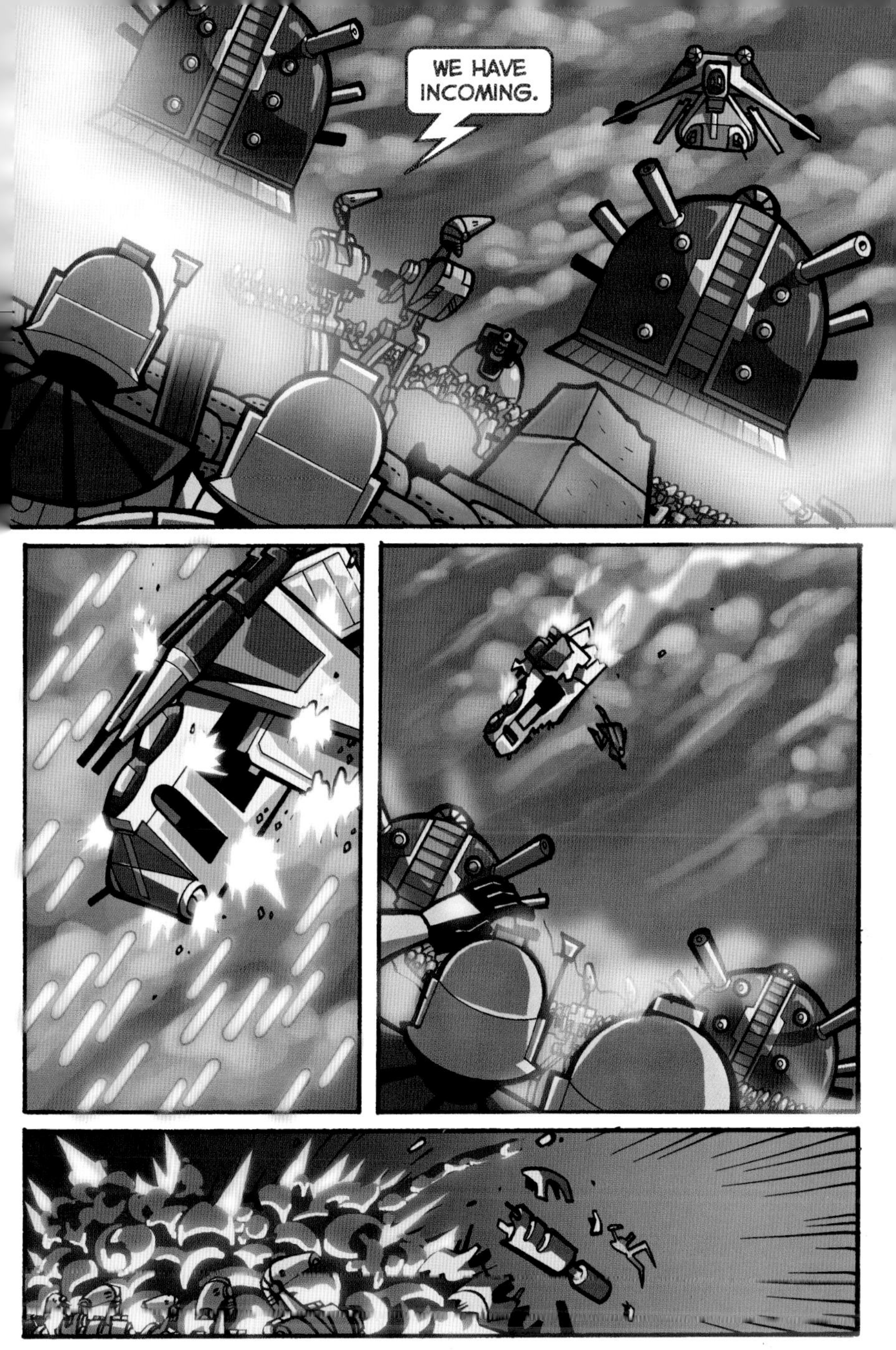
WE HAVE INCOMING.

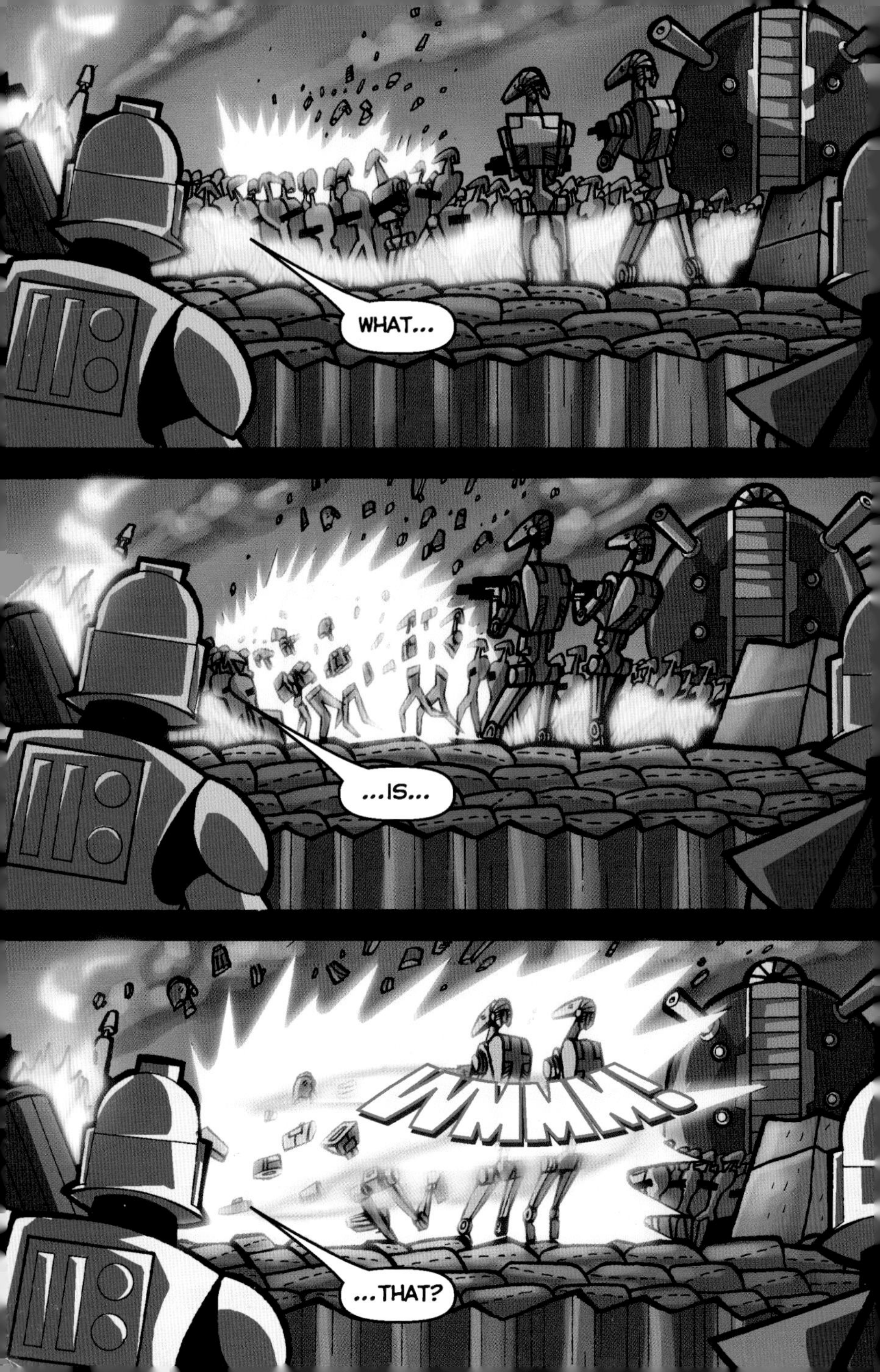
WHAT...
...IS...
VMMMM!
...THAT?

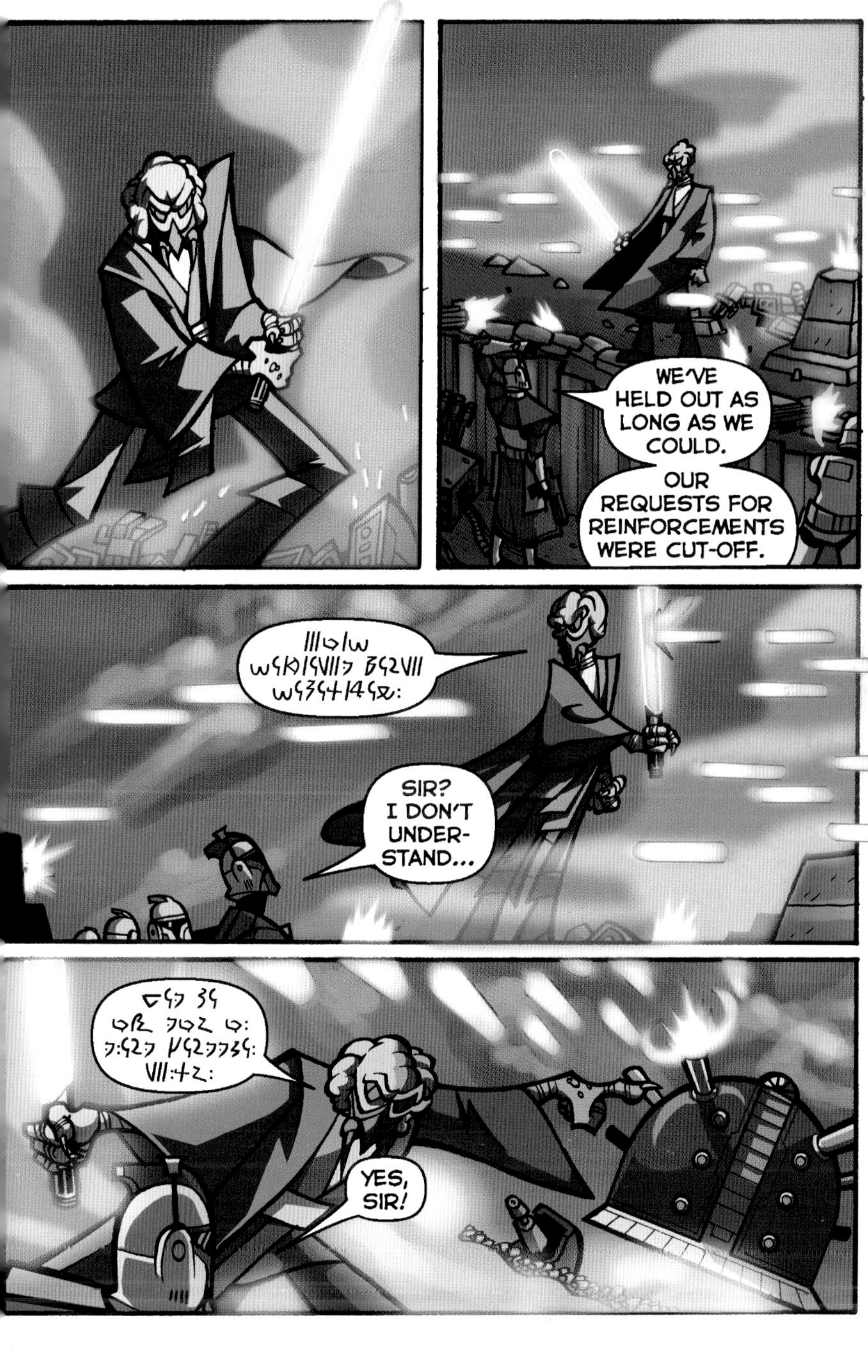
WE'VE HELD OUT AS LONG AS WE COULD.
OUR REQUESTS FOR REINFORCEMENTS WERE CUT-OFF.
SIR? I DON'T UNDER-STAND...
YES, SIR!

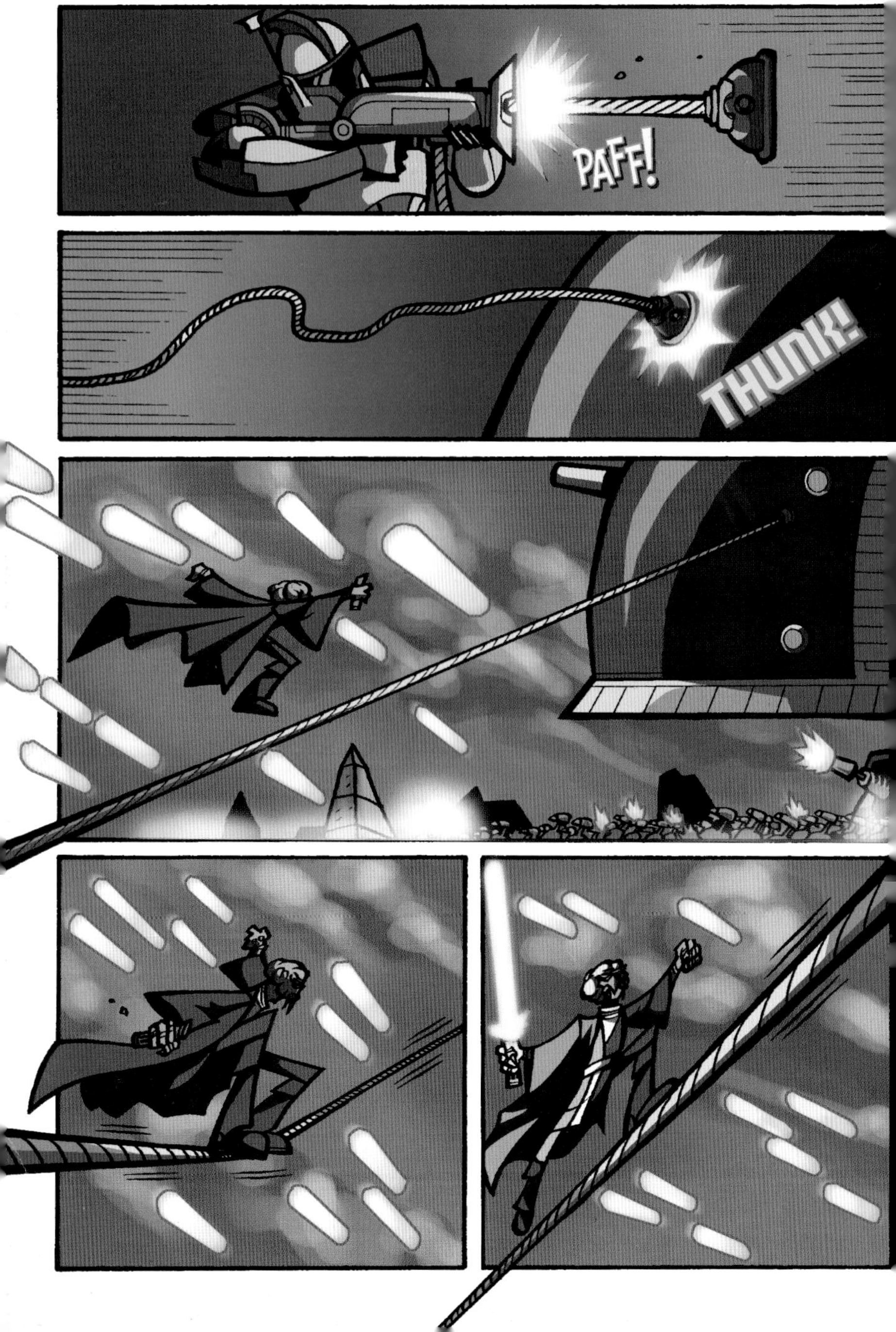
PAFF!
THUNK!

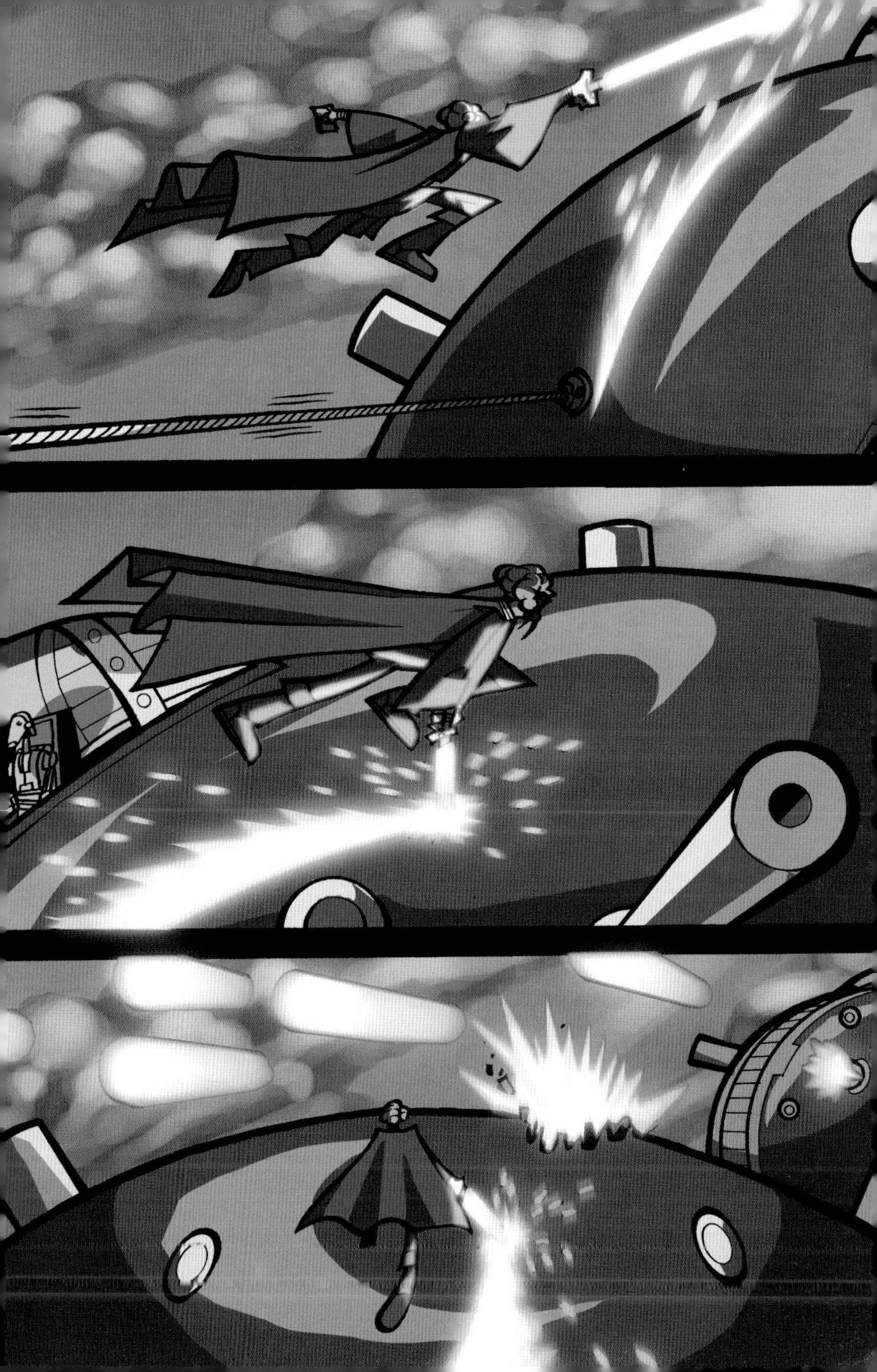

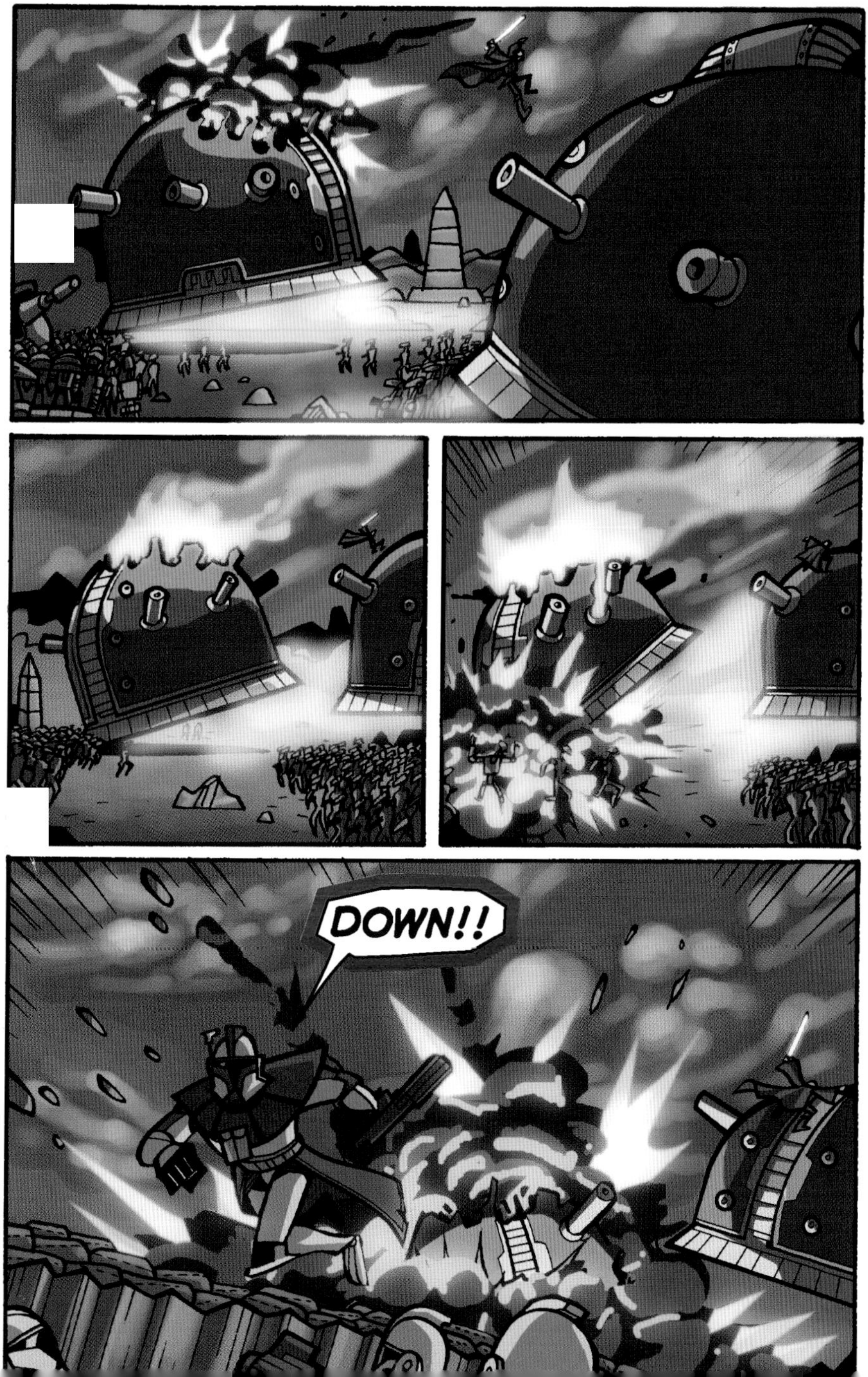
DOWN!!

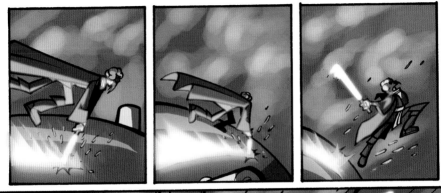

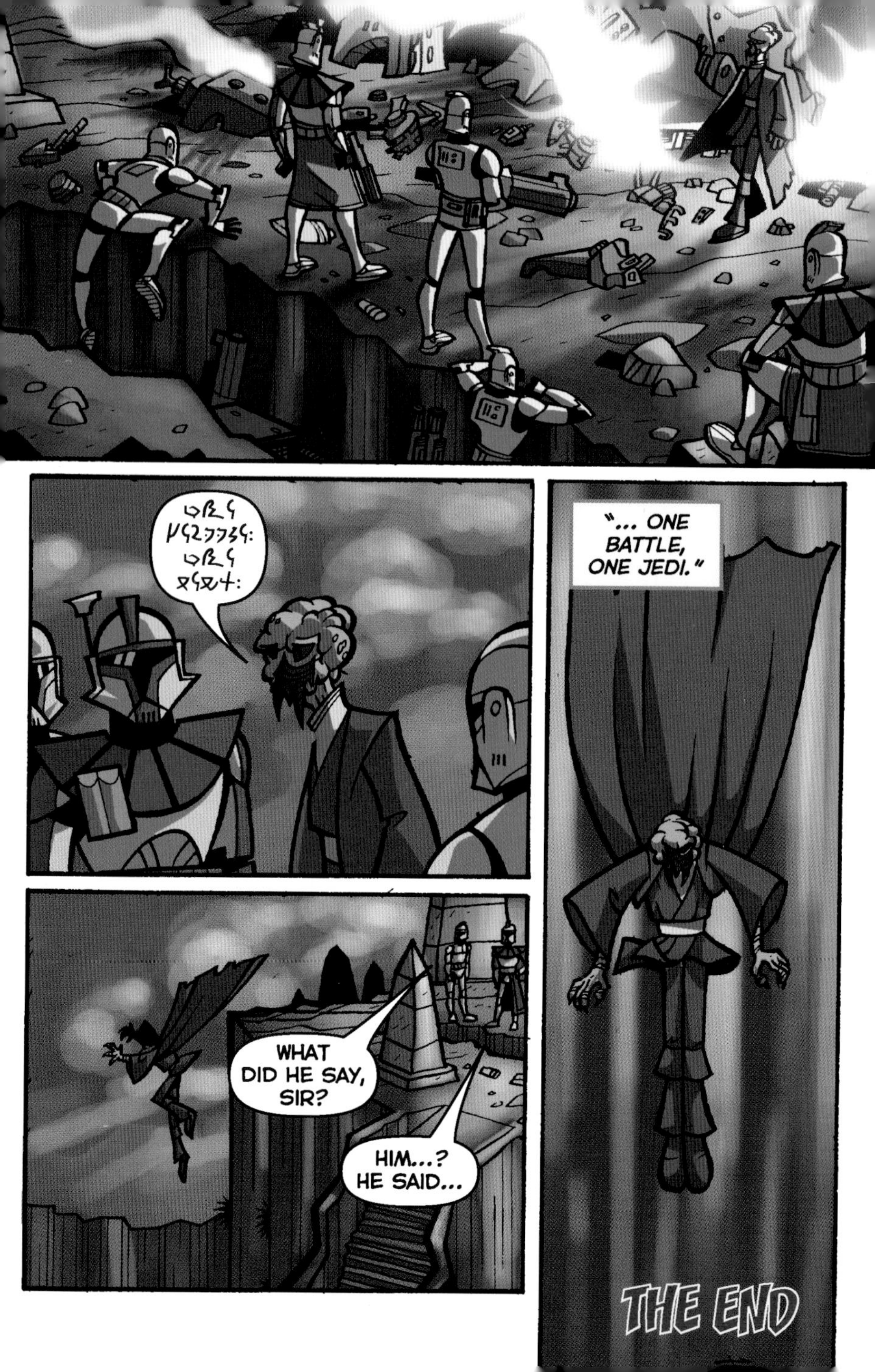

WHAT DID HE SAY, SIR?
HIM...? HE SAID...
"... ONE BATTLE, ONE JEDI."
THE END

STAR WARS®
CLONE WARS ADVENTURES

Don't miss any of the action-packed adventures of your favorite STAR WARS® characters, available at comics shops and bookstores in a galaxy near you!

STAR WARS
CLONE WARS
ADVENTURES
THREE NEW STORIES! ALL-JEDI ACTION!

Volume 1
ISBN: 978-1-59307-243-8

STAR WARS
CLONE WARS
ADVENTURES
THREE TALES OF HYPERKINETIC JEDI ACTION!

Volume 2
ISBN: 978-1-59307-271-1

STAR WARS
CLONE WARS
ADVENTURES
FOUR TALES OF SINISTER SEPARATIST SCHEMING AND ROCKING REPUBLIC COMBAT!

Volume 3
ISBN: 978-1-59307-307-7

STAR WARS
CLONE WARS
ADVENTURES
FOUR RIVETING ADVENTURES IN ONE FANTASTIC VOLUME!

Volume 4
ISBN: 978-1-59307-402-9

STAR WARS
CLONE WARS
ADVENTURES
FOUR AMAZING TALES OF HEROISM AND GALAXY-SHAKING ACTION!

Volume 5
ISBN: 978-1-59307-483-8

STAR WARS
CLONE WARS
ADVENTURES
FOUR TALES OF PLANETS IN PERIL AND JEDI IN JEOPARDY!

Volume 6
ISBN: 978-1-59307-567-5

STAR WARS
CLONE WARS
ADVENTURES

Volume 7
ISBN: 978-1-59307-678-8

STAR WARS
CLONE WARS
ADVENTURES

Volume 8
ISBN: 978-1-59307-680-1

STAR WARS
CLONE WARS
ADVENTURES

Volume 9
ISBN: 978-1-59307-832-4

STAR WARS
CLONE WARS
ADVENTURES
JEDI, CLONES, DROIDS, AND BOUNTY HUNTERS IN FOUR FANTASTIC TALES!

Volume 10
ISBN: 978-1-59307-878-2

$6.95 each!

To find a comics shop in your area, call 1-888-266-4226

For more information or to order direct: • On the web: darkhorse.com • Phone: 1-800-862-0052 Mon.–Fri. 9 A.M. to 5 P.M. Pacific Time. • E-mail: mailorder@darkhorse.com *Prices and availability subject to change without notice.

STAR WARS
CLONE WARS

Experience all the excitement and drama of the
Clone Wars! Look for these trade paperbacks at
a comics shop or book store near you!

To find a comics shop in your area, call 1-888-266-4226
For more information or to order direct:
• On the web: darkhorse.com
• E-mail: mailorder@darkhorse.com
• Phone: 1-800-862-0052
Mon.-Fri. 9 A.M. to 5 P.M. Pacific Time
*Prices and availability subject to change
without notice. STAR WARS © 2006
Lucasfilm Ltd. & ™ (BL8018)

READY TO TRY SOME OTHER GREAT STAR WARS® TITLES?

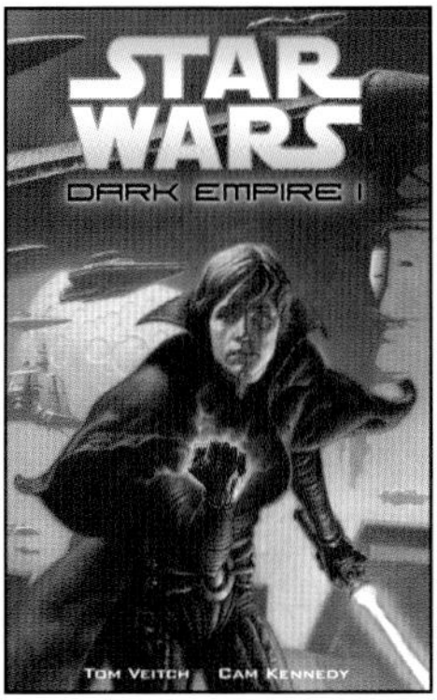
STAR WARS
DARK EMPIRE I
TOM VEITCH CAM KENNEDY

DARK EMPIRE

Join Luke, Leia, Han, and Chewie as they battle the Empire's latest super-weapons: the gigantic, planet-destroying World Devastators!

ISBN-10: 1-59307-039-X / ISBN-13: 978-1-59307-039-7

$16.95

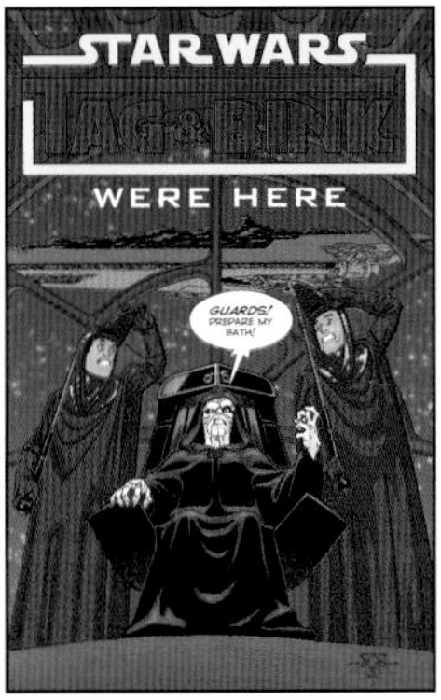
STAR WARS
WERE HERE
GUARDS! PREPARE MY BATH!

TAG AND BINK WERE HERE

Laugh yourself into orbit with the hilarious misadventures of a pair of hapless Rebel officers!

ISBN-10: 1-59307-641-X / ISBN-13: 978-1-59307-641-2

$14.95

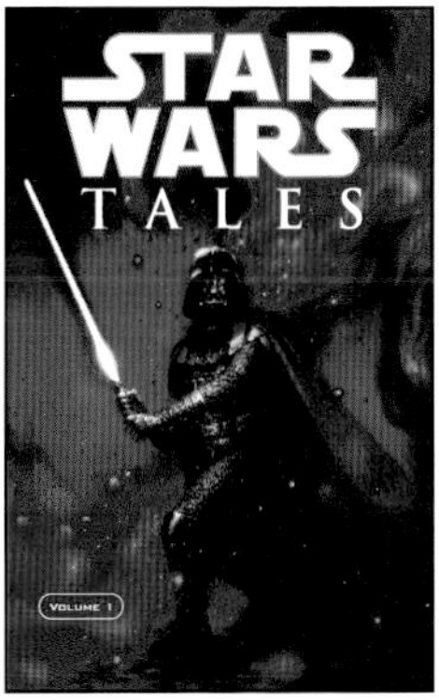
STAR WARS
TALES
VOLUME 1

TALES VOLUME 1

Read the first four issues of the quarterly anthology smash sensation that explores every corner of the *Star Wars* galaxy!

ISBN-10: 1-56971-619-6 / ISBN-13: 978-1-56971-619-9

$19.95

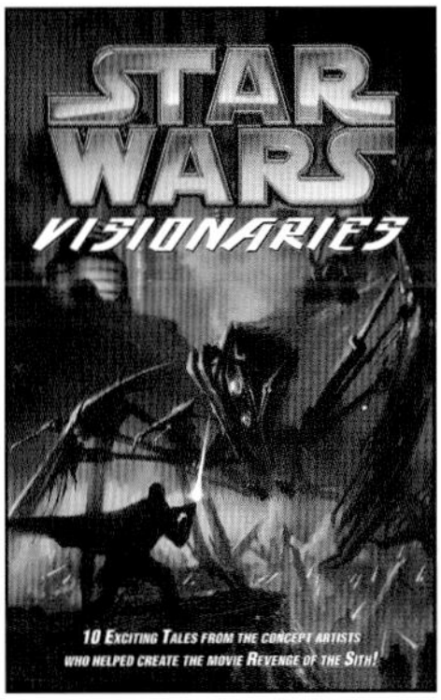
STAR WARS
VISIONARIES
10 EXCITING TALES FROM THE CONCEPT ARTISTS WHO HELPED CREATE THE MOVIE REVENGE OF THE SITH!

VISIONARIES

Ten exciting tales from the concept artists who helped create the movie *Revenge of the Sith*!

ISBN-10: 1-59307-311-9 / ISBN-13: 978-1-59307-311-4

$17.95

AVAILABLE AT YOUR LOCAL COMICS SHOP OR BOOKSTORE!

To find a comics shop in your area, call 1-888-266-4226

For more information or to order direct visit darkhorse.com or call 1-800-862-0052 Mon.-Fri. 9 A.M. to 5 P.M. Pacific Time.

Prices and availability subject to change without notice.

DARK HORSE | darkhorse.com | DARK HORSE TWENTY YEARS

COMICS | BOOKS | PRODUCTS | REVIEWS | ZONES | NEWS | HELP | COMPANY | RESOURCES

VISIT THE

ZONE ON DARKHORSE.COM
TO EXPLORE GREAT FEATURES LIKE:

- Exclusive content from editors on upcoming projects!
- Download exclusive desktops!
- Online previews and animations!
- Message Boards!
- Up-to-date information on the latest releases!
- A complete *Star Wars* timeline!

Visit DARKHORSE.COM/STARWARS for more details!

INDIANA JONES™

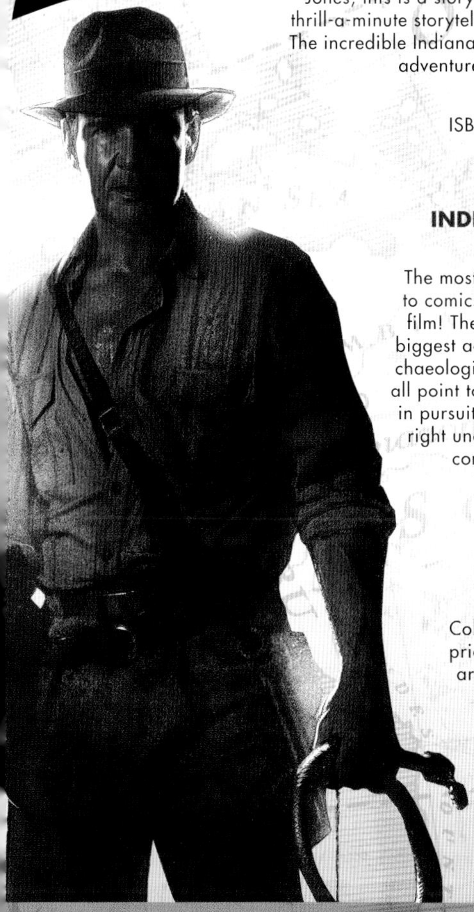

INDIANA JONES ADVENTURES

Kid-friendly and brimming with the very best parts of Indiana Jones, this is a story for anyone looking for stunning visuals, thrill-a-minute storytelling, and one unmistakable archaeologist! The incredible Indiana Jones undertakes an all-new, book-length adventure in this pocket-sized volume!

VOLUME 1
ISBN 978-1-59307-905-5
$6.95

INDIANA JONES AND THE KINGDOM OF THE CRYSTAL SKULL TPB

The most anticipated movie event of the summer comes to comics in this adaptation of the fourth Indiana Jones film! The intrepid Doctor Henry Jones Jr. is back in his biggest adventure yet! This time, the world-renowned archaeologist finds himself caught in a series of events that all point to a discovery unlike any other. But will his rivals in pursuit of this priceless treasure seize his quarry from right under his nose? Not if he, and a few unexpected companions, have anything to say about it!

ISBN 978-1-59307-952-9
$12.95

INDIANA JONES OMNIBUS

Collecting many long-out-of-print stories in value-priced volumes, *Indiana Jones Omnibus* collections are a perfect jumping-on point for new readers!

VOLUME 1
ISBN 978-1-59307-887-4

VOLUME 2
ISBN 978-1-59307-953-6
$24.95 each!

AVAILABLE AT YOUR LOCAL COMICS SHOP OR BOOKSTORE
TO FIND A COMICS SHOP IN YOUR AREA, CALL 1-888-266-4226
For more information or to order direct: • On the web: darkhorse.com • E-mail: mailorder@darkhorse.com
• Phone: 1-800-862-0052 Mon.–Fri. 9 AM to 5 PM Pacific Time. *Prices and availability subject to change without notice.

darkhorse.com

READY TO TRY SOME OTHER GREAT STAR WARS® TITLES?

STAR WARS
REBELLION
Volume 1: MY BROTHER, MY ENEMY

REBELLION VOLUME 1:
MY BROTHER, MY ENEMY

Imperial officer Janek "Tank" Sunber makes a critical choice between his duty to the Empire and his loyalty to childhood friend Luke Skywalker in an explosive tale of Rebel spies, Imperial ambushes, and the dreaded Darth Vader!

ISBN: 978-1-59307-711-2 | $14.95

STAR WARS
LEGACY
VOLUME 1 BROKEN

LEGACY VOLUME 1:
BROKEN

The Jedi Temple is attacked, an Emperor is betrayed, and the Sith are born anew! A lot can happen in a hundred years, but that's just the beginning of the story!

ISBN: 978-1-59307-716-7 | $17.95

STAR WARS
KNIGHTS OF THE OLD REPUBLIC
VOLUME ONE
COMMENCEMENT

KNIGHTS OF THE OLD REPUBLIC VOLUME 1:
COMMENCEMENT

Thousands of years before Luke Skywalker would destroy the Death Star in that fateful battle above Yavin 4, one lone Padawan would become a fugitive hunted by his own Masters, charged with murdering every one of his fellow Jedi-in-training!

ISBN: 978-1-59307-640-5 | $18.95

STAR WARS
DARK TIMES
Volume One: THE PATH TO NOWHERE

DARK TIMES VOLUME 1:
THE PATH TO NOWHERE

Jedi Dass Jennir and his companion Bomo Greenbark survived the Clone Wars, but the fate of Bomo's wife and daughter remains a mystery. The two friends are determined to find them, but their path leads them from danger to darkness—where each of them stands to lose more than they may hope to gain.

ISBN: 978-1-59307-792-1 | $17.95

DARK HORSE BOOKS

AVAILABLE AT YOUR LOCAL COMICS SHOP OR BOOKSTORE!

To find a comics shop in your area, call 1-888-266-4226.

For more information or to order direct visit darkhorse.com or call 1-800-862-0052 Mon.–Fri. 9 A.M. to 5 P.M. Pacific Time *Prices and availability subject to change without notice

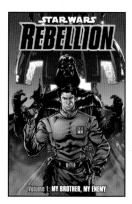

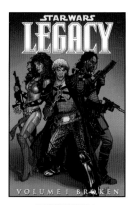

STAR WARS

TIMELINE OF GRAPHIC NOVELS FROM DARK HORSE!

OLD REPUBLIC ERA:
25,000—1000 YEARS BEFORE
STAR WARS: A NEW HOPE

Omnibus—Tales of the Jedi Volume 1
ISBN: 1-59307-830-0 $24.95

Omnibus—Tales of the Jedi Volume 2
ISBN: 1-59307-911-6 $24.95

Knights of the Old Republic
Volume 1—Commencement
ISBN: 1-59307-640-1 $18.95

Knights of the Old Republic
Volume 2—Flashpoint
ISBN: 1-59307-761-0 $18.95

Knights of the Old Republic
Volume 3—Days of Fear, Nights of Anger
ISBN: 1-59307-867-6 $18.95

Jedi vs. Sith
ISBN: 1-56971-649-8 $17.95

RISE OF THE EMPIRE ERA:
1000-0 YEARS BEFORE
STAR WARS: A NEW HOPE

The Stark Hyperspace War
ISBN: 1-56971-985-3 $12.95

Jedi Council—Acts of War
ISBN: 1-56971-539-4 $12.95

Prelude to Rebellion
ISBN: 1-56971-448-7 $14.95

Darth Maul
ISBN: 1-56971-542-4 $12.95

Episode I—The Phantom Menace
ISBN: 1-56971-359-6 $12.95

Episode I—
The Phantom Menace Adventures
ISBN: 1-56971-443-6 $12.95

Jango Fett
ISBN: 1-56971-623-4 $5.95

Zam Wesell
ISBN: 1-56971-624-2 $5.95

Jango Fett—Open Seasons
ISBN: 1-56971-671-4 $12.95

Outlander
ISBN: 1-56971-514-9 $14.95

Emissaries to Malastare
ISBN: 1-56971-545-9 $15.95

The Bounty Hunters
ISBN: 1-56971-467-3 $12.95

Twilight
ISBN: 1-56971-558-0 $12.95

The Hunt for Aurra Sing
ISBN: 1-56971-651-X $12.95

Darkness
ISBN: 1-56971-659-5 $12.95

Rite of Passage
ISBN: 1-59307-042-X $12.95

Honor and Duty
ISBN: 1-59307-546-4 $12.95

Episode II—Attack of the Clones
ISBN: 1-56971-609-9 $17.95

Clone Wars Volume 1—
The Defense of Kamino
ISBN: 1-56971-962-4 $14.95

Clone Wars Volume 2—
Victories and Sacrifices
ISBN: 1-56971-969-1 $14.95

Clone Wars Volume 3—
Last Stand on Jabiim
ISBN: 1-59307-006-3 $14.95

Clone Wars Volume 4—
Light and Dark
ISBN: 1-59307-195-7 $16.95

Clone Wars Volume 5—The Best Blades
ISBN: 1-59307-273-2 $17.95

Clone Wars Volume 6—
On the Fields of Battle
ISBN: 1-59307-352-6 $17.95

Clone Wars Volume 7—
When They Were Brothers
ISBN: 1-59307-396-8 $17.95

Clone Wars Volume 8—
The Last Siege, the Final Truth
ISBN: 1-59307-482-4 $17.95

Clone Wars Volume 9—Endgame
ISBN: 1-59307-553-7 $17.95

Clone Wars Adventures Volume 1
ISBN: 1-59307-243-0 $6.95

Clone Wars Adventures Volume 2
ISBN: 1-59307-271-6 $6.95

Clone Wars Adventures Volume 3
ISBN: 1-59307-307-0 $6.95

Clone Wars Adventures Volume 4
ISBN: 1-59307-402-6 $6.95

Clone Wars Adventures Volume 5
ISDN: 1-59307-483-2 $6.95

Clone Wars Adventures Volume 6
ISBN: 1-59307-567-7 $6.95

Clone Wars Adventures Volume 7
ISBN: 1-59307-678-9 $6.95

Clone Wars Adventures Volume 8
ISBN: 1-59307-680-1 $6.95

Clone Wars Adventures Volume 9
ISBN: 1-59307-832-4 $6.95

Clone Wars Adventures Volume 10
ISBN: 1-59307-878-2 $6.95

Episode III—Revenge of the Sith
ISBN: 1-59307-309-7 $12.95

General Grievous
ISBN: 1-59307-442-5 $12.95

Dark Times Volume 1—The Path to
Nowhere
ISBN: 1-59307-792-0 $17.95

Droids—The Kalarba Adventures
ISBN: 1-56971-064-3 $17.95

Droids—Rebellion
ISBN: 1-56971-224-7 $14.95

Classic Star Wars—
Han Solo at Stars' End
ISBN: 1-56971-254-9 $6.95

Boba Fett—Enemy of the Empire
ISBN: 1-56971-407-X $12.95

Underworld—The Yavin Vassilika
ISBN: 1-56971-618-8 $15.95

Dark Forces—Soldier for the Empire
ISBN: 1-56971-348-0 $14.95

Empire Volume 1—Betrayal
ISBN: 1-56971-964-0 $12.95

Empire Volume 2—Darklighter
ISBN: 1-56971-975-6 $17.95

REBELLION ERA:
0-5 YEARS AFTER
STAR WARS: A NEW HOPE

A New Hope—The Special Edition
ISBN: 1-56971-213-1 $9.95

Boba Fett: Man with a Mission
ISBN: 1-59307-707-6 $12.95

Empire Volume 3—
The Imperial Perspective
ISBN: 1-59307-128-0 $17.95

Empire Volume 4—
The Heart of the Rebellion
ISBN: 1-59307-308-9 $17.95

Empire Volume 5—Allies and Adversaries
ISBN: 1-59307-466-2 $14.95

Empire Volume 6—
In the Shadows of Their Fathers
ISBN: 1-59307-627-4 $17.95

Empire Volume 7—
The Wrong side of the War
ISBN: 1-59307-709-2 $17.95

Rebellion Volume 1—
My Brother, My Enemy
ISBN: 1-59307-711-4 $14.95

Rebellion Volume 2—
The Ahakista Gambit
ISBN: 1-59307-890-4 $17.95

A Long Time Ago . . . Volume 1—
Doomworld
ISBN: 1-56971-754-0 $29.95

A Long Time Ago . . . Volume 2—
Dark Encounters
ISBN: 1-56971-785-0 $29.95

Classic Star Wars—
The Early Adventures
ISBN: 1-56971-178-X $19.95

Classic Star Wars Volume 1—
In Deadly Pursuit
ISBN: 1-56971-109-7 $16.95

Classic Star Wars Volume 2—
The Rebel Storm
ISBN: 1-56971-106-2 $16.95

Classic Star Wars Volume 3—
Escape to Hoth
ISBN: 1-56971-093-7 $16.95

Jabba the Hutt—The Art of the Deal
ISBN: 1-56971-310-3 $9.95

Vader's Quest
ISBN: 1-56971-415-0 $11.95

Splinter of the Mind's Eye
ISBN: 1-56971-223-9 $14.95

The Empire Strikes Back—
The Special Edition
ISBN: 1-56971-234-4 $9.95

A Long Time Ago . . . Volume 3—
Resurrection of Evil
ISBN: 1-56971-786-9 $29.95

A Long Time Ago . . . Volume 4—
Screams in the Void
ISBN: 1-56971-787-7 $29.95

A Long Time Ago . . . Volume 5—
Fool's Bounty
ISBN: 1-56971-906-3 $29.95

Battle of the Bounty Hunters
Pop-Up Book
ISBN: 1-56971-129-1 $17.95

Shadows of the Empire
ISBN: 1-56971-183-6 $17.95

Return of the Jedi—The Special Edition
ISBN: 1-56971-235-2 $9.95

A Long Time Ago . . . Volume 6—
Wookiee World
ISBN: 1-56971-907-1 $29.95

A Long Time Ago . . . Volume 7—
Far, Far Away
ISBN: 1-56971-908-X $29.95

Mara Jade—By the Emperor's Hand
ISBN: 1-56971-401-0 $15.95

Shadows of the Empire: Evolution
ISBN: 1-56971-441-X $14.95

NEW REPUBLIC ERA:
5-25 YEARS AFTER
STAR WARS: A NEW HOPE

Omnibus—X-Wing Rogue Squadron
Volume 1
ISBN: 1-59307-572-3 $24.95

Omnibus—X-Wing Rogue Squadron
Volume 2
ISBN: 1-59307-619-3 $24.95

Omnibus—X-Wing Rogue Squadron
Volume 3
ISBN: 1-59307-776-9 $24.95

Dark Forces—Rebel Agent
ISBN: 1-56971-400-2 $14.95

Dark Forces—Jedi Knight
ISBN: 1-56971-433-9 $14.95

Heir to the Empire
ISBN: 1-56971-202-6 $19.95

Dark Force Rising
ISBN: 1-56971-269-7 $17.95

The Last Command
ISBN: 1-56971-378-2 $17.95

Boba Fett—
Death, Lies, and Treachery
ISBN: 1-56971-311-1 $12.95

Dark Empire
ISBN: 1-59307-039-X $16.95

Dark Empire II 2nd ed.
(includes *Empire's End*)
ISBN: 1-59307-526-X $19.95

Crimson Empire
ISBN: 1-56971-355-3 $17.95

Crimson Empire II: Council of Blood
ISBN: 1-56971-410-X $17.95

Jedi Academy: Leviathan
ISBN: 1-56971-456-8 $11.95

Union
ISBN: 1-56971-464-9 $12.95

NEW JEDI ORDER ERA:
25+ YEARS AFTER
STAR WARS: A NEW HOPE

Chewbacca
ISBN: 1-56971-515-7 $12.95

LEGACY ERA:
40+ YEARS AFTER
STAR WARS: A NEW HOPE

Legacy Volume 1—Broken
ISBN: 1-59307-716-5 $17.95

Legacy Volume 2—Shards
ISBN: 1-59307-879-9 $19.95

INFINITIES:
DOES NOT APPLY TO TIMELINE

Infinites: A New Hope
ISBN: 1-56971-648-X $12.95

Infinities: The Empire Strikes Back
ISBN: 1-56971-904-7 $12.95

Infinities: Return of the Jedi
ISBN: 1-59307-206-6 $12.95

Star Wars Tales Volume 1
ISBN: 1-56971-619-6 $19.95

Star Wars Tales Volume 2
ISBN: 1-56971-757-5 $19.95

Star Wars Tales Volume 3
ISBN: 1-56971-836-9 $19.95

Star Wars Tales Volume 4
ISBN: 1-56971-989-6 $19.95

Star Wars Tales Volume 5
ISBN: 1-59307-286-4 $19.95

Star Wars Tales Volume 6
ISBN: 1-59307-447-6 $19.95

Tag & Bink Were Here
ISBN: 1-59307-641-X $14.95

FOR MORE INFORMATION ABOUT THESE BOOKS VISIT DARKHORSE.COM!

AVAILABLE AT YOUR LOCAL COMICS SHOP OR BOOKSTORE
To find a comics shop in your area, call 1-888-266-4226. For more information or to order direct, visit darkhorse.com or call 1-800-862-0052 Mon.–Fri. 9 A.M. to 5 P.M. Pacific Time. *Prices and availability subject to change without notice.
STAR WARS ©2008 Lucasfilm Ltd. & ™. (BL8009)